SLOW COUNSELING

A relationship between two people
constellates a third—the relationship itself.
(Print by Nikki Schumann)

SLOW COUNSELING

*Emphasize the Healing Power
of Relationships*

Edited and Introduced by
David Tresemer, PhD

Lindisfarne Books | 2017

Lindisfarne Books
An imprint of SteinerBooks/Anthroposophic Press, Inc.
610 Main St., Great Barrington, MA 01230
www.steinerbooks.org

Thanks to Claus Sproll, Kaysha Korrow, and
Christy Korrow of Lilipoh Publishing (Lilipoh.com)
for encouraging this book in its early development.

Prints by Nikki Schumann used by permission
of artist, whose work can be seen at
www.NikkiSchumann.com.

Design, Jens Jensen
Cover photo © by Gabriel Cannon

Printed in the United States of America

LIBRARY OF CONGRESS CONTROL NUMBER: 2016956341
ISBN: 978-1-58420-975-1 (paperback)
ISBN: 978-1-58420-976-8 (ebook)

Contents

Slow Counseling: An Introduction

By David Tresemer

The notion of "slow" as a slogan and a movement began when Carlo Petrini in 1986 campaigned against a McDonald's fast-food outlet opening near the Spanish Steps in Rome. He couldn't bear to see that beautiful architecture—and steps by their nature slow you down—linked with the champion of "fast." He began the Slow Food Movement and wrote about his point of view in *Slow Food Nation: Why Our Food Should Be Good, Clean, and Fair.* In the country where a meal can last a long time, where taste is more important than stuffing in the calories you need to keep you going, where you smell the wine before you sip it and never gulp it, the notion of "slow" had found a home. Slow Food has taken root in many other countries, as well as the larger version, The Slow Movement, which has been applied to many aspects of human activity.

Our modern world has speeded up. It has become fast in so many ways. Why list those ways? You're in a hurry to get to the point, right? And for good reason, as the number of written words per year lifts to the stratosphere (if you put all the words end to end, they would indeed go there), and the incidence of half-baked ideas accelerates even faster. The truth is that good things take time. When I was younger, I lied about my age: "I'm nine...well actually eight and three-quarters," when I was a mere eight and a half. I was eager for life, eager to grow up. Maturation takes time; development of capacities takes time. The poet Horace said about poems, "Live with the poem for seven years," in which time you would read and revise. "If it has survived these transformations, then publish it." To the question, "What do you do?" the author Erma Bombeck answered, "I rewrite, then I rewrite again." We read and rewrite our lives, over and over again. Sometimes we meet bumps, and need some help to get over—thus the role of counseling.

I believe that everyone is counselor: aunt to nephew, police officer to kid on the street, lawyer to client, as well as licensed professional clinical counselor (LPCC) to addict. Any place where one human being comes to the aid of another, often simply by being there, qualifies as counseling.

The word *counseling* comes from two very ancient words, *com-* (together) and *-kel* (to call)—to call together in order to speak together. Thus, counseling's affinity to council and to counsel—for wise grandmothers, lawyers, and psychologists. The counselor honors the power of relationship and the medium of speaking, perhaps the most astonishing of the uniquely human traits. Inherent in speaking together is listening, ruminating, allowing a response to rise from the heart. Carlo Petrini would add, over fresh salad greens with organic olive oil, sniffing a glass of locally produced wine.

Professional counselors range from a young, hip, well educated man walking down the street with his adolescent client (see Gabriel Cannon's article on his preference for that setting) to licensed professionals who see a stream of very troubled people in their offices (various articles here). The professionals are challenged by a consortium of insurance companies, drug manufacturers, and even the government that demands they work faster, see more people, and assign those people DSM codes (from the *Diagnostic and Statistical Manual of Mental Disorders*) so that the drugs can be given out more quickly. As I describe in my chapters in the book *The Counselor...as if Soul and Spirit Matter*, the rise of this system is understandable, but it has gone too far. Robert Whitaker's excellent study, *Anatomy of an Epidemic: Magic Bullets, Psychiatric Drugs, and the Astonishing Rise of Mental Illness in America*, demonstrates that, whereas psychoactive drugs for depression or anxiety or social anxiety disorder may have helpful effects in the first few weeks, for many it's downhill from there. Compared to those who receive old-fashioned, talk-together counseling, the drugs do not fare as well. Whitaker warns that the "epidemic" of rapidly increasing numbers of those damaged by inappropriate use of powerful drugs will become in a decade an immense burden on society.

Whitaker asked the reasonable question, "What did society do before the advent of drugs?" By analyzing records from before the 1950s romance with chlorpromazine (Thorazine) and then Valium, and so on, he found that people experienced mental disability at the same rate as they do today and that, after a year, nearly all had gone home—back to work, back to school. It is our impatience—the fastness of life—that has caused us to start popping pills as soon as something has gone awry. Of course, we should not be too hasty in our judgment of pharmaceuticals. They certainly have their place, though likely not at the rising rates that we see today. Whitaker's warning is well researched and well worth reading.

Things speed up, and everyone has more of those things, all going faster. For the most part, we get used to the speed. Scientists predicted that going fifty miles per hour in the new thing called a railroad train would create serious mental disturbance. It didn't happen. We got used to that speed. Yet we never accounted for what we lost. If you walk a route, or even part of a route, that you normally drive, so many other experiences become available to you. Every so often you need to do that. Not to cease driving, or using phones or computers, rather to insert into your lives a balance with slower. Things speed up, and when you become too speedy, you become a thing—both client and counselor.

The contributions assembled for this volume on slow counseling range widely, appropriate to an art that shows up everywhere that humans show up to help one another. The volume begins with a piece I wrote for *Lilipoh* magazine on anthroposophic psychology. Psyche, Greek for soul: the go-more-slowly understanding of the human being, rather than the human seen as merely a collection of genes and chemicals. Logos, patterns observed in the soul. Anthropos, the possible human being; Sophia, the divine feminine wisdom that underlies all of this wondrous creation. Soul and spirit can't be defined, which frustrates the ones who like to measure things. But here's the catch: Not only can't they be defined, they ought not be defined, for their nature is fluid and alive.

Next come two pieces from anthroposophic psychologists in India and Argentina, followed by the vibrant and natural counselor, Heidi Rose Robbins, who is in real life as radiant as she writes.

Then I interviewed Beatrice Birch, who founded Inner Fire, devoted to giving a place for those wishing to go off their medications, ending with a verse that she chose from Rudolf Steiner. Cynthia Taylor writes about using counseling methods in a school setting.

I include a poem by Susan Lanier, because in very few words it shows the kinds of sensitivities that a counselor can develop that cannot be developed when you're seeing clients at twenty minutes apiece. Clairvoyance (the *clair* part also comes from the old Proto-Indo-European *kel-*) is something that most people have experienced, though these skills remain undeveloped. Note in this poem a learning moment, that the clairvoyance is much deeper than expected. This twist made this poem very attractive to include in this collection.

Claudia McLaren Lainson's piece speaks to an issue in which many people believe—possession by forces unseen—though it is rejected by mainstream scientists. However, read this piece to ascertain the integrity of the counselor for yourself. Gabriel Cannon's piece also speaks to the situation of young people, and the need to engage authentically with them.

Lila Sophia Tresemer has written a companion piece to her book, *The Conscious Wedding Handbook*, talking about how old relationships, though over, linger and should be dealt with. No matter how you try to avoid the passing relationship—now you can break up with another via an internet service who will for a fee send the other an "It's over" text—old relationships take time to dissolve. Following this is a collection of six short columns that I wrote for *Lilipoh* magazine on a problem with alcohol that serves as a platform for discussing many aspects of anthroposophic psychology.

Jennifer Stickley, herbalist, natural healer, and student of anthroposophic psychology, offers a profound perspective on the foundations of a full life, illustrated by an art piece by her friend Benjamin König.

Micheal Hooker leads us through her approach to counseling via performance art. Dave Heap writes about slowing down and including a counseling component in physiotherapy. Margit Ilgen, also in the training for anthroposophic psychology, writes professionally about depression.

Finally, I give a poem about point of view, about a journey following the leads that are there. In my view, the eagerness to solve the riddles of humanity sometimes leads to premature closure, and this poem recommends that you take your time, slow down, and enjoy the process.

Nearly forty years ago I wrote *The Scythe Book: Cutting Weeds, Mowing Hay, and Harvesting Small Grains with Hand Tools*. It sells every year about a thousand copies. People are interested in taking the time to enjoy their every moment, including their every chore. The point of that book is that slow is fine if you have good tools to accomplish those tasks, tools that don't hurt you in the process. I hope that this book will be a helpful tool for you to slow down in your counseling, both the giving and the receiving.

A note about the front cover: The cover photograph shows one person with a hand on the shoulder of another. Though this should be celebrated as an emblem of the healing power of relationships, this behavior has come under attack, and is now legislated by governments and licensing bodies for professionals. This simple gesture of touch is especially scrutinized by the teaching profession. From the point of view of effective counseling, touch should be included—a simple touch on the shoulder can be an extremely powerful moment in a journey of healing, learning, and relating. Your local or professional government may prohibit such behavior, in which case, you will have to learn how to radiate warmth and intimacy from your own being.

Anthropos Sophia Psyche Logos

By David Tresemer, PhD

The twelve syllables of "anthroposophic counseling psychology" give you a mouthful...but to know those twelve syllables is to love them. Besides their meaning (at the end of this article), there are good reasons to know about anthroposophic psychology (AP) as a growing field of inquiry and practice. A recent meeting of the international association of associations at Emerson College (Forest Row, England) had representatives from teaching institutes of AP from India, Israel, Italy, Spain, the Netherlands, Germany, Spain, England, Argentina, Brazil, Japan, and the US. The United States was represented by the Association for Anthroposophic Psychology (AAP). All of them are linked to the Medical Section in the School of Spiritual Science of the Anthroposophical Society in Switzerland (which has requested that the term *anthroposophic psychology* be used instead of *psychosophy*).

Two books have recently appeared in English that lay out the foundations of AP. Ad Dekkers, with his wife Henriette Dekkers, has given us *The Psychology of Human Dignity*, now translated into English. They are responsible for the founding of most of the AP trainings in the countries mentioned. The Dekkers' expertise is the creation of exercises to show the dynamics of the four bodies foundational to an anthro-posophical understanding of the human being: the physical (more complicated than what you normally assume), etheric body or body of rhythm and habits, astral body or body of thoughts and feelings, and the I-AM wherein we can say "I am; I exist." It takes time to differentiate these, but then you've got an important tool of understanding.

The other recent book is *The Counselor...As If Soul and Spirit Matter*, edited by me (with contributions from William Bento, Edward Knighton, and Roberta Nelson). It takes the position that counseling occurs in many settings: an aunt speaking with a niece, a "licensed addiction counselor" (LAC) with a recovering addict, also lawyers, life coaches, wedding planners, policemen, ministers, indeed anyone engaged in a whole-soul conversation...which includes everyone. An introductory section of *The Counselor* lays out AP in relation to other traditions of psychology. Though the book is over three hundred pages long, chapter 1 gives three dozen aspects of AP that haven't been covered in the book, and which the authors have taken on as a challenge for the future. The next section, Fundamentals, begins the process of presenting the foundations of AP, in this volume with chapters on the phases of life. (Isn't it amazing that we live so many lives within one life? These can be understood in seven-year segments, and AP can help understand the different qualities of these different lives.) The next section reformulates the mainstream clinical issues of depression, addiction, trauma (including post-traumatic stress disorder), and the personality disorders as given in the bible of conventional psychology and psychiatry, the *Diagnostic & Statistical Manual*, version five. A final section speaks to the inner development of the counselor, a topic often neglected in texts and trainings.

AAP has begun trainings in different parts of the United States, each nine seminars long, a process taking three years for personal and professional enhancement, through individual and group explorations, through concepts and experiences. Rudolf Steiner gave annual lectures on the psychology of body, soul, and spirit in 1909, 1910, and 1911. He clarified and expanded upon these concepts here and there up to World War I, when the chaos of world events interrupted that direction of inquiry. Why has it taken so long for these ideas to be gathered together and developed into a coherent approach related to mainstream psychology? Steiner predicted this rhythm when he said that ideas sometimes require an incubation of a hundred years. Here we are a hundred years later, and it's exciting. And it's just in time as conventional psychology is rapidly moving toward pharmaceuticals and formulas-for-right-thinking-straight-from-the-manual. The notions of soul and spirit have been neglected, shunned, and insulted. AP seeks their return, not as magical woo-woo, but as deep transformative experiences that lead to growth in relation to the human individual's purpose for living.

Now for the syllables of AP, starting at the end. I give these in greater length in *The Counselor*, but this will give a taste. Logos—the pattern, the "logic" of the story, never meant as dry intellectualism, but rather as finding an order in the mish-mosh. Psyche, Greek for soul. Thus psychology, the story of the soul in its structure and in its journey.

Counseling, from the Proto-Indo-European for together (*kom-*) speaking (*-kele*), which in combination with Anthroposophy means whole-soul conversation.

Sophia, sometimes known as Greek for wisdom, the feminine principle of creation. Encountering this principle goes far deeper than a pretty image of Mother Nature "over there." It goes to the experience of one's being within creation itself "in here." I thank Sophia for loaning the elements for my body so that I may live and move and learn (a matter of profound meaning for me, as I express with my wife at SophiaLineage.com).

Anthropos, often translated "the becoming human being" or "the possible human being." Here I'm being mysterious, but that's because it's a mystery: Anthropos as the divine template from which all individual human beings are drawn, who has a pan-individual intention to link with Sophia in a process of mutual transformation. Thus Anthropos-Sophia, not only a mouthful, but a life-full, and quite likely many lives full.

Counseling—in India

By Parimal Pandit

Once upon a time, India was the land of holiness and abundance, a land where truth was revealed by a slow transformation of the human spirit, where saints modeled the importance of patience and genuineness thorough devotion. Over time it was consumed by materialism and the motto "the more the better." It succumbed to fast food, fast lanes, fast cars, fast work.... And India forgot to breathe.

As with many health and healing modalities, even counseling and psychotherapy took over the "instant" and "short term" labels. In India the more traditional couch therapies had never really taken strong roots as in Europe or Ameriaca. NLP, CBT, and REBT became the more popular modes of counseling and psychotherapy.*

However, interest in spirituality, psychology, and counseling is growing. Those in the fields of technology and IT say, "I don't have time. Give me something now quickly, a solution to end all my troubles. Jaldi! Jaldi!" Yet the psyche is speaking back.

---

* Even the names have become shortened so you can say them more quickly. NLP is neurolinguistic programming; CBT is cognitive-behavioral therapy; REBT is rational emotive behavioral therapy.

The beauty of creating new relationships and developing them, establishing inner harmony, waiting and letting the new relationship marinate to make the feelings more tender, and giving time to slowly unfold the different realms of yourself and the other person, is mostly lost. In my counseling I must bring the element of slow and subtle transformation of an individual through work on self-revelations.

One thing I learned and observed in my counseling career is that if we prioritize and work on one aspect at a time, it helps the clients to learn to trust this process. I work with patients or clients over three to four months. As they transform, gain control, and feel empowered by their inner strength, they stop running.

The process is as spiritually rewarding for the client as it is for me. From the beginning I used to wonder if anything existed that is beyond the visible. I discovered that as you go deeper in the therapy, it comes to address the core existential questions that lie beyond the observable. How to reach that is up to the counselor. For example, a client came with a panic attack at the age of forty-two years. After working on the anxiety for over three months, we started working on reaching the stage of detachment. He continued to come for therapy for more than five months, and his questions changed from "why" to "how do I attain this capacity to be sensitive yet not get drawn in by my emotions?" In the language of anthroposophic psychology, he began to transform his astral body and to bring what was unconscious into consciousness. This all came about through working on his own biography, working on his "double" (that familiar yet rejected part of us that is derived from our most difficulty life experiences) through art and through his own yoga practice.

Anthroposophy can help in bridging the gap between here and now to the space beyond time. This takes courage. As a psychotherapist I had always tried to look beyond. Such an adventure has no short cuts, though anthroposophic psychology helps to illuminate the path there. When I work with clients, I look to see if the person is ready for more. Is he or she looking for more? Or perhaps I concentrate only on the problems at hand. For example, a client continues to struggle with anger and needs only anger management techniques. I utilize traditional psychotherapeutic techniques. I also introduce artistic painting to work on reining in the astral body and on bringing the "I" into deeper expression. For example, I used charcoal on paper with a teenager struggling through his parents' separation, trying to deal with his anger toward his father. It worked wonders with him finding his own ground. A boy who had been shy in expressing himself could stand up to his father to say what he felt; he could stand by his mother as a support. It took time but he worked it through himself. He was fifteen years old when he came to me. This process helped him in the process of incarnating his will.

Slow is what helps the individual thorough transformation. It need not all happen here and now during the period of counseling. You see the ripple effects where the client continues to discover himself/herself that will continue afterward. It has begun here in these counseling sessions.

From India we bring the gift of transformation and transcending, the gift of accommodating and amalgamating of cultures, of patience and of fortitude; we bring forgiving and healing to the field of counseling, and all this in its own "slow" time.

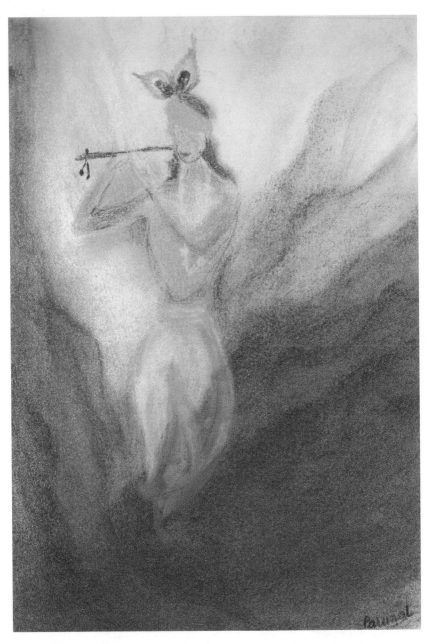

Krishna *by Parimal Pandit, a composition for a Krishna devotee. It shows the transition of magenta to purple: prebirth (magenta) to afterbirth (purple). Someone is there with you before your birth and after.*

Krishnajayanthi is important in India and where I work at the institute for special children, who can easily become little Krishnas pushing you to your destiny, testing, teasing…they can also help you to rein in the astral forces.

ADDENDUM

Chennai, the city I reside in, witnessed torrential rains and flooding recently. The heavens literally opened up and we saw the worst deluge seen in the past hundred years. Thousands lost everything they possessed. It spared no one, neither rich nor poor. All the differences in society were treated equally by nature. Many companies lost their properties, their goods damaged. Many big IT firms had to be shut down, lowering their production. Many lost their dear ones. Out of this Pralaya (the drowning) emerged muck, garbage, and selfishness. Much more than those dark forces, the golden hearts of people emerged, who opened their homes and hearts, and helped day and night in rescue and relief operations. All people big and small, whatever they could pitch in, helped. We discovered lost relationships when networks shut down for four days; electricity shut down for a week. The counselors were overburdened with the many people who needed our help. Yet we could see our clients, the children, discovering hidden talents, speaking, mingling, helping, sharing food. We saw an immense amount of warmth arise, which we had lost in this fast world. Many blame urban development, materialism, and consumerism for this destruction. Yes, in a way everywhere on earth we experience this. But it's heartwarming to see that through it all, the power of warmth still exists and can still be kindled if only we allow ourselves that.

Anthroposophic Psychotherapy

By Inés María Iturralde

What does it mean to "go slow" in modern times? From my point of view the important thing is the depth of the encounters between therapist and patient.

A deep encounter crosses time and space. When deep, a moment condenses into something that lies in space and develops in time.

It is important to respect the power of time for a process to develop. That process does not respond at once to an imposition from outside. The process has its own laws and forces, and should be left to act, for a real transformation can then occur.

Patience and waiting: These are two words that indicate realities that we must permit to work within each of us.

We must learn to wait, until it is possible to extract from the process of time that which we have matured. The important thing is what lies in the hearts of therapist and client, after that "ripening time." Forces grow there that propel one forward.

How is that depth achieved?

In the encounter between two people, we allow Spirit to approach this sacred space. Something new appears that neither the therapist nor the patient knew. A new meaning appears.

This implies that the therapist must have confidence in the process.

The meeting between therapist and patient is a karmic encounter. This meeting produces warmth that comes from the soul and spirit.

We learn from the seriousness of this knowledge that the treatment cannot hurry; it will last that has to last.

The interest of the therapist in the patient's life has an effect on treatment. What matters is the quality of that meeting, it cannot be perceived when the emphasis is on "fast and superficial."

The therapeutic space is a sacred space where at least two people meet. This meeting of souls allows the Spirit to work. It enables the work of the Spirit of the people involved in the treatment and the Spiritual Being who ensures that treatment.

This is possible through respect and understanding of people and processes. This understanding comes naturally from within all human beings.

The rapid and fleeting encounters of short treatments can only achieve superficial and external changes. The human being is not an object that can be managed from outside.

In an anthroposophic worldview, the human being is a psycho-spiritual being, embodied in a physical body governed somewhat by heredity. The human being lives between these two currents, between heaven and earth.

The encounter between therapist and patient is a deeply spiritual encounter. It is a karmic encounter. In that sense it is sacred.

It Takes Time

By Heidi Robbins

It takes time. It takes time for a friendship to be nourished, for a house to be built, for a book to be written. It takes time to make a beautiful meal, make a card for a loved one or write a poem. Love takes time. Creativity takes time. Growing into who we truly are takes time.

I have been an astrologer and poet for over fifteen years. I have a one-on-one practice and I also lead retreats for women. My practice has grown slowly and deeply. My circle of clients is large but also intimate and true. I have invested in each relationship and I have seen those relationships bloom.

As a student of astrology, I am interested in cycles and right timing. Though I am happy to do a single reading for a client, I am always most interested when I get to work with a client over time and watch her navigate the darker hours and thrive during times of light.

Slow Counseling is the only kind of counseling that makes sense to me. I often work with poetry during my retreats. I read to the women. I read slowly and watch as the words pierce their hearts, as they take the time to listen to something deeply. I watch as something opens within them that could not have opened if we weren't breathing together, listening together and offering ourselves to an organic and nourishing pace.

Often when I am working with a client or teaching at a retreat, I will simply stop and allow us to be in the silence together. I think of it as a kind of digestion time. It's a time when we don't know what's next and when we are allowing assimilation of what has been shared thus far. Silence affords us crucial synthetic time.

When I meet with clients over a number of years, it is a great joy to watch them grow more and more embodied. That is, I can see that the wisdom is living within them. Their process has become a joyous process of self-discovery and not a search for the "right" information. They are proactive, radiant, curious, and at peace with the pace of their lives. Working with clients over time, in an organic rhythm, creates an opportunity to build intimacy and trust which are essential for growth. Nothing happens overnight and if it does, there will still be necessary adjustment time to such rapid growth. Self-compassion, quiet, contemplation, and assimilation will still be necessary.

In an age where everything and everyone moves at an increasingly rapid and unceasing pace, it seems to me that Slow Counseling honors the most natural rhythms in our body—the beat of our heart, the quiet inhalation and exhalation, the need for sleep and the need for activity. It honors the seasons within our body and the seasons in the world. There is time. There is time to grow. There is time to experiment. Life is not a rush to be hurried through.

One of the greatest joys of my Radiant Life Retreats is the fact that twenty women spend four days together—sharing meals, living in community, having tea early in the morning, and taking walks together. We come together in a time out of time and leave behind what defines us "in the real world." We show up and work to cultivate something new within ourselves—a quality of being, courage, a desire for connection. There is nothing to do but breathe and grow and encourage one another. There is nothing to do but play and nourish ourselves and speak of what matters.

In an online world, it's becoming more and more the norm to meet through technology rather than in person. But humanity needs touch and presence, the warmth of a hand or the kind eyes of another. The deepest nourishment and the greatest opportunity for growth comes through presence, a deep well of listening and true connection. May we all find a pace and texture that allows us to unfold more deeply and completely into our truest selves.

Beatrice Birch on Slow Counseling

By Beatrice Birch
in conversation with David Tresemer

DT: I would like to ask a question that's been burning inside and that is: What is the spark of inner fire?

BB: I would call it our divine creative self. Due to medications or an imbalance that happens because of trauma, for example, we can lose touch with that creative self. Without our inner fire, it's very difficult to recover from life's debilitating and traumatic experiences.

DT: Do you feel that you're on a mission to help people find their inner fire?

BB: To help them recognize and reconnect with it, yes. I've certainly met people where you can say there's only a flicker of that inner fire left. But, it's amazing, when they feel the love that I have for them, the belief and interest in them as a creative human being and not a label, something begins to shift. It's like watering a dying plant. Something begins to stir within and I can see it almost straightaway in their eyes.

DT: What does that mean, not a label?

BB: Nowadays when you're having some difficulties and you see a psychiatrist, within a few minutes they're going to label you as this or that in order to then be covered by the insurance companies, by Medicaid, or whatever. This label has nothing to do with healing.

DT: That's a strong statement. The label has *nothing* to do with healing? Are you standing by that statement?

BB: Yes, I'm standing by it. Labeling somebody just so they can be medicated when you've only known them for ten minutes and maybe then another ten minutes in a month or two's time... too many psychiatrists have no idea what is going on, on a deeper soul level, therefore they have no idea as to who the person before them really is. Many struggling individuals experience labeling as a stigma, they feel misunderstood and boxed in. The fact that an individual even comes for help means that on some level or another, they are seekers and they are looking for support. Medications tend to disguise and suppress the essential challenge. On the other hand, people are misled by being told that the chemistry in their brain is out of balance.... There is no difference in the brain if someone is labelled as schizophrenic, bipolar, or depressed. These are not a disease such as diabetes.

DT: I know you use the word "seeker" in your work. What does that mean?

BB: I have been working in a couple of prisons for a number of years and one day a young man approached me who was in one of my painting classes. He said to me: "I was trying to write to a friend on the outside about this art class and it's so hard to describe what happens. Eventually I wrote to my friend: 'it's an art class, but it's really a spiritual class.'" And then he said to me, which is key: "This is what I was looking for on the outside. Isn't it strange I had to come to prison to find it?" I realized right then: "You, like so many other people, are a seeker; you're looking for something more than this fast-paced, superficial, materialistic life which has disheartened and alienated too many sensitive and striving people." People are being controlled and swallowed up by the pressures and pace of life, rather than they themselves being able to have some influence in the directions of their lives.

DT: In a prison the label would be "criminal." A psychiatrist would use other kinds of labels. What are some of the labels that are used most often these days?

BB: Bipolar, schizophrenic, obsessive compulsive, manic, anything along this line. New labels are being invented daily. Some people are labeled with four or five different labels. Symptoms change due to the side effects of the medications so the seeker soon is on a cocktail of medications. Naturally the person is wondering: "Who am I? Am I really just that label? Isn't there more to me than that?" Oftentimes nobody will listen to the seeker. The parents and the case managers too often believe what the psychiatrist says, ignoring their own intuitions. For the seekers, it's an incredibly lonely experience. Nobody believes them. No one listens to them.

DT: So actually the label becomes a greater reality in the eyes of others than the seeker himself or herself?

BB: Typically yes, though in time, doubt can seep in and the seeker may begin to wonder, for example, if indeed, the chemistry in their brain *is* wrong. And for those people who have been labeled this way, they consider it a stigma. Then, of course, they feel that "nobody meets me for who I am and who I am striving to be;

no one will listen to the reasons why I have fallen into this life situation." Again, we look so superficially at the extremely complicated and mysterious human being.

DT: The labels do have usefulness though, don't they, in terms of speaking to insurance companies and getting support for your treatment?

BB: Getting support from the insurance company is linked with medications. But an alternative to the medications is as yet not supported by the insurance companies to any serious measure. Clearly the intentions of the insurance companies and pharmaceutical companies are interwoven. We need insurance companies to support a proactive rather than passive engagement of the striving individual. In the long run the costs are lower because people can actually recover and not remain on disability. But clearly, this would be bad for the business of the pharmaceutical companies. People have forgotten that the human being has a body and also a soul and a spirit...that's I think one of the key mistakes...we're looking at the human being more and more as just a physical body which we can tweak and manipulate. We forget or deny that on a deeper soul level there may be something that may have become incredibly out of balance because of trauma. The real healing comes when trying to bring that balance back again.

DT: I sense that you're using trauma in a very broad way. Is that correct?

BB: Yes. Well, in quite a general way. You could say that a human being is repeatedly falling in and out of balance. Efforts at "being human" accompany us daily. Notice that "being human" is a verb, an activity. The way we can gain support in getting back toward a kind of a balance is crucial. But there always seems so little time for that; mistakenly, people are looking for quick fixes, magic bullets.

Here's an example. I know a woman who was born into a third generation of child trafficking in East London. She was abused from the age of three. She coped as best she could, but it was particularly when she had her own child that her voices started to speak to her of what a horrible person she was, that she was not worth being a mother, that she should jump out of the window....

After many tormenting years, she was able to address her inner voices: "You must feel awful to speak to me like that. Nobody who is happy talks like that to anyone else..." Her voices totally changed. Honestly, which of us having gone through abuse like that beginning at such an early age (only three years on this earth...), would want to be in that body? We all have our coping mechanisms. That's an example of trauma.

Trauma is also relative. For some people it could be something so simple that others would find it a joke, but for that person it is incredibly traumatic. A lot of the children I've worked with over the years, I've had to say to parents: "There's nothing wrong with your child. Your child just hasn't toughened up as quickly as other children." Many parents will tell me: "My child was known as the sunny child—generous, enthusiastic, warm, sensitive, curious ..." Isn't this what we would ideally want for any child? Then in those vulnerable teen years things began to happen. Often marijuana or some form of pot which is laced with something far worse comes into the picture. Marijuana is not what it used to be back in the 1960s. Often, these poor children can't get back into their bodies after such experiences. More often than not the people who come to me are around the age of twenty-two and they've had some kind of traumatic experience, often with drugs. And the parents tell me of the child's life, how they were so open and sensitive to begin with.

DT: They couldn't handle the many repeated traumas of modern life?

BB: Yes. Look at education nowadays…little children have the stress of passing tests to get into kindergarten. What are we doing to our children? Why at that age should they be under such pressure? We need to wake up and acknowledge what is happening to childhood and do something about it. When do they have the opportunity to simply play together and learn how to interact socially without competition?

DT: These people find you in their twenties. What in your view is the task of the counselor for them?

BB: The task of the counselor is, first of all, to take a very deep interest in the person who is in front of you—"Who are you? What are your gifts? What are your aims? What do you want to bring to this life?" That's first.

DT: I have to interject here that you can't do that unless you've applied that same warm interest to yourself.

BB: For sure. Love is the key. You know, at some conferences where I have presented and referred to Love, some seem to take it as a joke or even embarrassing. It's referred to as "the L word." Certainly every counselor must love the other person...to say it like that sounds too superficial, but I am serious. In your heart, you have to know why you are doing this work as a counselor. What stirs you? Is it love, love for the striving human being? Do you recognize the individual before you as a creator rather than a victim? Granted, we all can feel a victim at times....

If your job is simply linked to your paycheck, then forget it. Sorry. I have to be completely clear if we are really looking for healing.

For over thirty years I've been offering Hauschka Artistic Therapy. What I have grown to realize is that when someone walks into the room and when they begin to work under my guidance with the artistic therapy, I am looking for what I call the "divine, creative self" in that person. It's there. Creative work continues as they establish a deep connection with the creator within—their self image begins to change; harmony begins to arise on this deeper soul-spiritual level. There need be little outer conversation, because it's an artistic process, it's slow. It's the process that counts.

Over and over again people say to me, including the seekers in prison, that they totally forget where they are and that time flows so differently. Their breathing changes and deepens. Talking does have its place, but often many clever folks repeat the same thing to their numerous counselors...they know they're repeating themselves. I have often experienced their relief when I ask for more depth, acknowledging their challenges and strivings.... It is important to actually empathize with what they've gone through in their life.... Part of counseling is to be able to identify with what they have gone through without becoming it. Identify with and empathize, realize that must have been hell, and not become it yourself.

You are more than your trauma—that is key. We can see our traumas and our hiccups in life as simply part of our life tapestry: I would say ideally we would have many different colors in our tapestry, some deep, dark or hard colors, some rich and soft colors of light—a whole spectrum of colors—this makes for a rich tapestry of life. It is also empowering to acknowledge that our challenges are there to keep us growing, they are not meant to overwhelm us but we may need to stretch out of our comfort zone.

DT: Tell me about your Inner Fire project in relation to these ideals that you have been speaking.

BB: For about twenty-five years or so, I had been working in anthroposophical medical and therapeutic centers in England and also in Holland. When I came back to the United States, I was horrified to see how people were so easily medicated. I started working at a rehabilitation center in Vermont. And one day, a young man came in to me and said: "I've got all these feelings going on inside me and I can't reach them. I used to be able to think clearly, but I can't anymore. It's as if the meds are pushing who I really am under the table."

I agreed with him. He looked at me and said: "Nobody in fifteen years has ever agreed with me." He started doing remarkable artistic work. I was even told he had an IQ of a five- to seven-year-old, which is total rubbish. He was actually playing the game: "If you expect me to be stupid, I'll be stupid. But if there's somebody who will treat me as a human being with respect and interest, we can have very interesting conversations." That's what happened. One day I looked out the window and saw him jogging, which was totally unheard of for him.

Soon after, he came in and plunked down at the table and put his head in his hands. I asked: "What's up?" He said: "The doctor changed my meds." I almost started crying. I couldn't believe it. This man had progressed so far. I asked him: "What meds are you taking?" And he said: "I don't know." "What do you mean you don't know?" He looked at me, the fire was burning within him at that moment and said: "I hate being medicated and nobody listens to me. My parents don't listen to me. The psychiatrist doesn't listen to me. The case managers don't listen to me. So the easiest thing to do is just to take the meds."

Through him the grapevine began to work; more and more people started coming to me and standing in front of me, saying: "I hate being medicated, isn't there a choice?" I was in the position of either having to lie and say, "No dear, take your meds," or risk my job and say: "Yes, there is a choice...."

Meanwhile, there were seekers who had been at this rehab, who were discharged, and then had committed suicide. Some of them I had worked with and hated the thought of them leaving, feeling they're not ready, nothing has really happened for them. And after the sixth suicide, I just thought "Enough, I can't go on—I can't go on knowing that this is happening."

I approached my husband Tom, who has been a tremendous support, and others. I realized we had to offer the choice I was so aware of from my years of practicing in Europe in anthroposophically rooted medical and therapeutic centers and other alternative rehabs. I knew what we could do to help Seekers strengthen their soul spiritual self while helping heal their physical body by easing off their medications. I see the suicides as sacrifices that individuals made to help us awaken to the epidemic overwhelming and smothering the individual human spirit. Inner Fire simply is offering the choice too many individuals have been seeking yet were never aware of. Let me describe the program.

Before officially opening the Inner Fire Program in September 2015, we'd had two nine-day sanctuaries, where individuals came to have a taste of what it would be like to be at Inner Fire. Rhythm is crucial. How can there be any inner order if the outer life is chaotic? Breakfast is at 7:00. (Before arriving, they had to practice getting up at 7:00 and going to bed by 10:00.) Breakfast is followed by a short morning walk. We then review the day. The seekers work for blocks of time in either the kitchen, biodynamic garden, forest, or in housekeeping. Naturally, diet is very important for health and so the seekers learn to cook properly with organic and local ingredients. We are essentially following the GAPS diet which helps to strengthen the flora of the gut.

After lunch every seeker receives a liver compress—the liver is the organ that deals with toxins. In the afternoon there are proactive therapies three times a week, Monday, Wednesday, Friday—therapeutic eurythmy, spacial dynamics, massage, music, speech art, Hauschka artistic therapy, and biographical work. The therapies that the seeker engages in are particularly appropriate for them; it's not a random selection, but it's looking at that person's situation and what he or she needs.

Tuesdays and Thursdays are allocated to peer work as well as biographical and psychosynthesis work.

Each evening a different cultural activity happens. For instance, on Mondays seekers have made their knitting needles and are learning to knit. Another evening, seekers listen while a biography is read to them. Many young people have the feeling that they should be perfect straight away. There's a polarized black and white picture so prevalent today in the United States: "I have to know it; I have to be a professional as soon as I get out of college." Biographies depict a journey and are therefore so valuable because they show the ups and downs and the twists and turns of life, in other words, the process of being human. Singing is also invaluable as we learn to listen to each other and learn to harmonize. Drumming, meditation, free-art sessions, evenings of appreciation, and evenings sharing a question about the world as we each learn to speak out. Weekends we are often out hiking, exploring the beautiful green mountains of Vermont.

Inner Fire is a year-long program. During the year, each individual has the opportunity to make a pair of felt slippers, carve a spoon, make a doll, a drum, and a book. These they will use and take with them when they leave.

Upon graduating from Inner Fire, we want to make available a Creative Living Community, which would mean an eight- or ten-bedroom house in Brattleboro in which our seekers can live and practice what they have learned at Inner Fire—practice the cooking, practice the gardening, practice the housekeeping. We are looking for someone who would like to start such a small business of renting rooms to our Seekers.

We have a wonderful blacksmith and glass blower working with our seekers during the winter months and I hope to find other crafts and trades people to mentor our Inner Fire apprentices. Before leaving Inner Fire, if wished, the seeker will connect with one of these crafts or tradespeople and work with them for two, three, or five days of the week, whatever is appropriate. Meanwhile, they may hold down a part-time job or do some volunteer work in our neighboring and vibrant town of Brattleboro. Of course, the seekers are always welcome to come back to Inner Fire on weekends to join in and inspire those striving to also strengthen themselves at a deeper soul spiritual level while detoxing their physical bodies from the cocktail of psychotropic medications.

DT: That's a beautiful picture. Will your seekers be going off of their medications when they join you?

BB: Yes, actually, Inner Fire is really about *Choice*. What someone chooses is their business. Some folks are perfectly happy on their medications yet too many others have committed suicide because they are not aware of the choice. Inner Fire is for people who want to be proactive and come off their mind-altering psychotropic medications. If you're happy on your medications, then you don't really need Inner Fire. We will have only twelve seekers at a time. When they first come, the most important thing is rhythm. Out of form comes freedom, and that should really be taken seriously. There is a rhythmic order to the day.

    Depending on the seeker it might be a month or six weeks before they are secure in their rhythm, then very slowly we can address the withdrawing of medications. Our psychiatrist's main role is to help people come off the meds. As one is detoxing the physical body, you need to strengthen the soul-spiritual self. The therapies and the work program are about strengthening the soul-spiritual self while the physical body is being detoxed.

DT: I'm struck by how you're working with time. This is a book on slow counseling and you're talking about the program taking a full year. And even after that, having a kind of halfway house where the seeker can practice what he or she has learned. You have also mentioned how, when someone is in an artistic activity, they lose a sense of time, they loosen up about time. I contrast this with the emphasis on fast results that is presently in our mental health arena and in the culture in general. Do you have any comments on that?

BB: When I first told the Board of Inner Fire that this is going to be a year program, one of the Board members stated: "No one will ever stay for a year." My response was that this is false economy. I know so many youth who have gone in and out of one rehab after another for quick fixes, for which the parents pay astronomically. It's a waste of time, precious time; it's a waste of money; and it's demoralizing for the human being. No deep and lasting healing is quick; it is a life process. Living fully is about falling in and out of balance and growing from these experiences.

In contrast, we offer the possibility to just be here, just be and *engage*. Even though the day is full, it's not fast. It's full, it's rich, and everybody will engage in the way that they can engage. It's not about doing the job perfectly. It's doing it as best as you can at this time. I believe so sincerely that in time, a seeker will get better at what they commit to. Really believing in a process is so important, and that's terribly lost these days where immediate results are expected.

DT: Do you have any final comments on this wonderful interview?

BB: Yes. At this time, the most painful part of this whole process for me is when I get three or four phone calls a day from all over the country and, after sharing of their longing and their feeling of hope at the prospect of coming to Inner Fire, the question comes: "How much does it cost?" At Inner Fire, we are struggling to make this available to people regardless of their financial situation. I believe so strongly that health is a right. It is not a privilege. Coming to Inner Fire should have nothing to do with money. For years I have been working with extraordinary men in two New York prisons; Inner Fire needs to be an option for them as well as those who are more privileged. I know a woman whose son took his life because he hated being medicated and saw no other option than to live his life in a fog of medication. The medications were inhibiting him from proactively dealing with the source of his challenges. After a couple of years, I approached her and asked: "Would you ever be prepared to give another young person the opportunity your son never had?" She said, "Yes." One of our seekers is very grateful for her generosity.

So, we have to be creative. Money must not be a reason for seekers not to come to Inner Fire. That means "it takes a village." I receive phone calls and emails from seekers or parents of seekers from across the country and internationally as far afield as Australia who state that though they personally may not be able to come due to the costs, the fact that Inner Fire simply exists is encouraging and catalyzes hope. We need people who believe that Inner Fire should be more available and who can help generate monies for our Support a Seeker Fund. There are some people who believe that Inner Fire will spread like wildfire once it starts and once people see what it takes to really deeply heal. We'll see, we'll see.

DT: May your new initiative thrive in service to the world. Thank you.

Addendum from BB: Inner Fire has just graduated its first six seekers. Everyone who came on medications is now off. And they are reclaiming their lives. Here is an abbreviated account by a parent: "After a seven-week stay at the psychiatric ward, the hospital released our daughter into our care, but she was on very high doses of antipsychotic medications and was not able to function on her own. [Then she came to Inner Fire.] The phenomenal and consistent care, love, patience and support from all the core staff members and the support team at Inner Fire, the daily regular rhythm of scheduled activities and responsibilities, the regular schedule of sessions in a variety of therapeutic modalities, the physical outdoors activities, the peaceful beauty of the environment, the camaraderie and support among the seekers, the delicious, wholesome and therapeutic diet plus too many other factors to mention, all created a space for our daughter to slowly begin to trust and to find and discover herself.... Inner Fire saved our daughter's life."

Beatrice Birch asked that this verse from Rudolf Steiner be added to this interview.

Love is for the world
what the sun is for outer life.
No soul could live
if Love departed from the world;
It is the moral sun of the world...
to spread Love over the earth,
to the degree possible;
to promote Love—
that alone is Wisdom.

The Role of the Counselor
in the School Setting

By Cynthia Taylor

In a school, the goal of educating the students should unite parents and teachers—and, for that matter, the whole community. Most of the time this unity occurs. Sometimes it doesn't. Conflicts inevitably arise. My job as pedagogical administrator (from pedagogy, the teaching of children), which in my opinion is a form of counselor, is first to listen.

A mother knocks on my door, barely able to conceal her anger about how her child is being treated by the child's teacher. The child has special needs and, according to the parent, the teacher isn't acting appropriately toward those needs. On the school outing, this and that occurred. I listen. The anger has at its base a mother's protection for the child. Mama Bear has come out. My job is to help the parent and then the teacher see the other's point of view. This takes time.

Not only parents erupt. When teachers feel disrespected, misunderstood, and sometimes insulted, they sometimes want to quit, as of today.

In a Waldorf school and community, we realize that much more is going on than what is assumed in mainstream education: These encounters occur because of long-term working of the soul of each and every one. Teachers, parents, administrators, and students who join a Waldorf community swirl in a maelstrom of karma and destiny. A teacher might feel strong antipathy for a particular student. The teacher must delve deep into his or her own soul life to explore this relationship, because this is not the first time teacher and student have met. How can we open ourselves to the realities that flow from the far past and the far future but are inaccessible to our physical senses in the present? Encounters between individuals in Waldorf communities can be very intense, yet we try to understand them as having a much longer past and future.

"This school is not big enough to contain both of us" is a statement that has been cast between different individuals in many Waldorf communities. The result is often that one or more people leave the community with hurt feelings, confusion, and bitterness remaining in the wake of the split. We are drawn to our community in order to grow in Spiritus, in our capacities of soul and spirit.* Can we begin to do this more consciously, moving toward healthy relationships?

In any school, as in most institutions, the life of the community is built upon relationships. For better or for worse, each individual has a role to play in the whole. The health, or lack thereof, of the school community is dependent on the health of its individual members and their interactions. How can good health be intentionally fostered in this kind of community? Is it even possible to generate health consciously in a constantly changing group of people? A school can fall apart

---

* EDITOR: The reference to capital S *Spiritus* comes from chapter 1 of *The Counselor... As if Soul and Spirit Matter,* wherein the task of mainstream psychology often seems to be the desire to reduce the sufferings of Pathos, whereas another dimension is more important for soul work, the degree of development of soul and spirit—*Spiritus.*

because no one anchors everyone in reality; misunderstandings erupt and are never dealt with in relation to facts and mutual understanding.

When I first arrived in Kelowna six years ago to take up my duties as administrator and teacher, I had little idea about what is involved in the administration of a school and a body of people. I came to realize that my role was not paperwork, but rather counseling relationships. I learned about the history of the school community; I learned to create relationships with many people. Reflecting back over the years I have the feeling that all the tough times I have had and all the difficult people I have been forced to live with during my life have given me the exact capacities and strengths that I needed in order to be able to do my work now, in this setting. My task has largely been to create harmony and stability in our community.

How can the wisdom of this knowledge be brought by an anthroposophic counselor into the school community in a tangible way?

A school community, or any community for that matter, can be perceived as an entity with a biography, and spirit beings that guide it. Studying the biography of the school by looking carefully through its history can bring much insight into present inner workings. How old is the school? What seven-year life stage is it in? Is it a child? An adolescent? An adult? Look at the school's time line and examine the ups and downs. What is the nature of the crises that have manifested in the past? A careful study of this kind can illuminate helpful clues about what is happening in the present. Long- and short-range planning might be done more consciously when community members are aware of tendencies, strengths, and a feeling for what is and will be needed.

Similarly, the daily interactions and relationships of the individuals and the group can be more objectively observed in relationship to the seven life processes. These are: a.) breathing or taking in, b.) warming, or adapting, c.) nourishing or penetrating, d.) sorting out or individuating, e.) maintaining or sustaining, f.) growing, and g.) generating. Not everyone is fully functional in all these areas. We can work together much better if we can recognize that some people are better at taking in new information, some at adapting it to fit in with what they know, and some at penetrating it with their intellect. Others may be better at generating something new and creative. Members of a group can work with each other's strengths to build a better whole.

The counselor coming from Anthroposophy can ask important questions about the work of the group as an initiation process. Where are we on this path? How do we move forward together? How do we each fit in? What holds us back? What strengths do we have? Do we love each other? The counselor can empower the group to create its pathway to healing, through thick and through thin, through self-examination and growth as individuals and as a group. In short, the counselor can help the group to grow toward Spiritus.

There are many ways an anthroposophic counselor can help the parent community as well. Parenting programs can be enriched as if soul and spirit matter. Parents often need help and guidance in raising increasingly willful children. Parenting can seem like a minefield; the counselor can help parents to find a less explosive pathway through it. Conflict resolution and discipline are often challenging areas where our emotions can get the better of us. It is beneficial to have someone present who can remain objective and guide the process to a happy outcome for all. I talk with the Mama-Bear mother protecting her cub; I listen. I talk with the teacher of the mother's child; I listen. The most important gift I bring is my listening, complete listening. Not taking sides, rather listening. My listening promotes patience for all. After a time, we can meet as a threesome.

No one person can take care of the needs of everyone, the counselor included. Each member of the community has strengths and capacities. As we get to know one another, we begin to recognize these strengths in each other. I sometimes think my main job is to ferret out and acknowledge the special abilities of different community members. I have learned to empower individuals, which has the dynamic effect of creating enthusiasm and positive action instead of festering discontent. It feels good to be useful and recognized as skilled at something. It also feels good to be heard. I have learned many ways to let someone know that they have been accurately heard. These skills can be learned and practiced with the help of the counselor.

Perhaps the most important aspect of building health in community is the cultivation of inner peace. The place to begin to create health in any community is inside one's self. No amount of effort at tackling discontent and negativity in the outer world will succeed in bringing harmony to a community if I have not inner peace. As long as I myself remain reactive and fearful, ill health in my community is inevitable. How can a counselor have any influence on the inner world of community members? To begin with, it is part of the learning process of becoming a counselor to delve deeply into one's self in order to identify one's false beliefs and to generate inner health. A counselor who has done this work extensively will have attained a degree of peace in his or her inner world. The power of one individual's inner peace in relation to a community cannot be overestimated. The inner peace of one person radiates outward into the entire community and has a positive influence. I have seen this again and again. To my amazement I have observed my own inner peace spread out like a ripple on a still pool, affecting a whole community.

How does this work? A person who is not fearful will usually not direct their energy toward negative things that they cannot control. When community members get caught up in parking lot gossip or speculation—I never imagined before taking this position that the parking lot would be such an active forum—or when they react emotionally to an event (that may or may not have happened), the counselor remains in a place where he or she can encourage people not to feed the negative spiral that results. The counselor who is able to remain at peace is also able to make quick, rational decisions when the need arises. It is very important in a school community to have leaders who are willing to take responsibility. Leadership is more effective if it comes from a place of inner peace. Thus the counselor becomes a person to whom others are drawn for advice or support. I cultivate the capacity to give others my undivided attention, expressing empathy, and enabling the other to realize his or her own inner strength. The counselor thus acts as a reflector of inner peace, radiating strength and confidence into the entire community.

In any group of people working together, transgressions occur between individuals. During times of stress, people react to each other with strong emotions. It is very important for these individuals, and those affected, to take time to cool off before taking action. The counselor can be of great assistance in helping people to take a few breaths. All parties can be encouraged to sleep on it and come together in the morning, or, if need be, take a few days to think things over. The opportunity for forgiveness is opened up for those involved. Much social destruction can be avoided through skillful intervention. Our interactions can take on a higher quality if we become able to rise out of our emotions and act more consciously.

Coming from a place of inner peace, the counselor is also able to use humor to ease tension and create positivity. Laughter is truly good medicine. It can soothe shattered nerves, change the mood, create a positive starting place, help people to see themselves in a new way, and help to relax tense muscles, particularly in the face. A community that laughs together stays together. The counselor can help to remind people of this. Regular playing of games is also a good practice that can be encouraged by the counselor. Creating opportunities for physical play is an important counterbalance to sitting at meetings. Without the counselor there might be no one to consciously monitor the level of tension, exhaustion, and isolation that individuals are feeling.

I have another technique that has been very helpful. I have been inspired by creation stories in Anthroposophy about the origin of everything, and the divine beings who were involved in that. Of course, as with all creation stories, these are difficult to know personally; however, they can be imagined. Every year, around the dark time of Christmas, I make twelve watercolors of my imaginations of these divine beings. I use the technique of veil painting, repeated coats of dilute colors, letting the forms slowly emerge from the page. I frame the paintings one at a time, and put up one each month in the

Cherubim, Spirits of Harmony

Thrones, Spirits of Will

faculty meeting room. The simple power of color is enough to sustain us through some challenging meetings. The stories are invoked, too.

The more colorful relates to the Spirits of Harmony, exploring the virtue of selflessness. The study in blues was inspired by the Spirits of Will. I see in this one a tempestuous night, one man reaching out to another in a hopeless state, to draw him toward the shelter offered by the small cottage. In this I feel the power of will becoming courage.

As we get caught up in the duties and responsibilities of our job and role, we must not lose sight of each other. It is too easy to say, "I don't have time," when someone wants to talk, go for a walk, or have dinner together. Individuals can easily feel isolated and become hopeless or depressed. It becomes easy under these circumstances to feel separated from each other. We must learn to consciously check in with each other. Nothing else, in fact, is so important as the brotherhood/sisterhood that needs to be nurtured between humans. It is the anthroposophic counselor's task to keep the heart-to-heart dialogues in our awareness, alive and active, with sincere caring. It is in this kind of working together that we truly bring spirit into matter. If a faculty can cultivate inner peace and heartfelt, caring relationships, and work out of a common spiritual bond, then the healthy relationships thus created will foster similar relationships throughout the community. This conscious activity raises human beings closer to spiritual beings and radiates into the cosmos as a healing for humanity.

The Gift

by Susan Lanier

the vet at the wildlife sanctuary
requested I read the young fox

who'd been found by the side
of the road I sat on the floor

beside his cage and did
an intuitive scan I recorded

his bruises and broken bones
a slight concussion

she asked if I thought
he was in immediate danger

no I said no he could wait
until morning for surgery

but he died overnight
the vet told me I had

misdiagnosed him
but strangely had described

precisely the injuries of the fox
who'd previously occupied

the same cage I mourned this
young fox until I realized he

had revealed
to my well intentioned scrutiny

not his weakness
but his vital skill as fox

to double back
through space and time fearlessly

One Day at a Time: John's Long Journey

By Claudia McLaren Lainson

As the final minutes of our third session ticked away, I sat there wondering to myself: "What are we doing here?" I couldn't find a window into the soul of the young man—I will call him John—sitting opposite me in my consultation room. John was very polite, even talkative, as if we were sharing afternoon tea. Then it happened. Simultaneously the young man before me imploded and exploded. He collapsed into himself, throwing his face into his hands, pulling at his hair, scratching his face, sobbing uncontrollably, gasping for breath, stating over and over again: "I don't want to end up in jail!"

His shattering rippled through me as rivers of agitation flooded into the room, conveying one simple message: In each psyche, only a fragile divide separates states of coherence from states of madness.

I stayed with him calm. I walked with him through his hysteria, after which he could communicate his dilemma. John had different people living inside his head and they were tearing him to pieces. This was my first experience with dissociative personality disorder (formerly called multiple personality disorder). John could no longer endure the complexity of his dissociation. He could no longer control the behavior of the others, nor even remember what they had said or done. Thus he was repeatedly confronted by friends, teachers, and parents who would accuse him of things he had no recollection of doing. Insanity was luring him to the edge, where peace was promised if he would only plunge off the precipice into the neverland of an illusory freedom. Such freedom of the insane is gained by surrender of the self, which is the defeat of reason; ultimately the "I" is sacrificed upon an altar not set up by the good powers. John was fighting to not "jump into the abyss" despite the magnetic pull the adversaries were exerting on him.

After John had retrieved a semblance of centeredness, I managed to pass him off to his mother without confiding to her his condition. This confidence in me was immensely important to John; it was absolutely necessary for his healing. If he was assured privacy, he could keep open the door between coherence and madness; his true self could continue to battle for his soul against the netherworld that was calling out to him. If he had to add the weight of parental fear to his already very precarious balance, the scales may have tipped, landing him outside of his mind—lost in the incessant chatter of the "others" indwelling him. A feather-weight balance of consciousness stood between the two possible directions before which he was standing, as his destiny delicately hovered above, awaiting his choice.

What the mind attends to determines what will grow, and there are collective thought forms that must be overcome in this process. Pharmaceuticals cut off the lows as well as the highs, making it more difficult to swim away from the swirling vortices of mass thought patterns that exert a tremendous power on the human psyche, just as a sinking ship draws those in its vicinity into its power.

In this case the mass thought pattern was dissociative personality disorder. If I fed this, he would likely sink; if I nourished the imagination of his wholeness, he would be restoring that in him which could mend what early trauma had rent asunder—his divine selfhood.

With John's permission, I called a psychiatrist who specializes in dissociative disorders. She guided me through the process of "making contracts" with John to ensure his safety until he met with her. I gave John's mother the psychiatrist's name, recommending she set an immediate appointment with her.

All I could tell John's mother was to watch him carefully, ask no questions, and give him space—a tall order for a parent who sees her child's level of distress, smells the prickling warnings of danger, and feels the piercing arrow of fear as it enters the heart. I encouraged her and her husband to have faith in the strength of their child. I let them know I was there if they needed me. Well, I thought, of course they wouldn't. This is not my area of expertise. I felt confident, though, that the situation had been placed in the right hands. The anxiety John's episode caused in my soul, could be allayed—or, so I thought at that time.

The next day I received a call from John's mother, who had just returned home from the psychiatrist's office. She told me John was adamant that he would not go back to see this woman, nor would he go see any other doctor. He was very clear on two things: that he would see only me, and that he did not want medication.

My therapeutic training embraces the notion that those who come to us for healing actually bear healing gifts for the healer. Such a perspective serves to kindle a deep interest in the holiness of the relationship between therapist and client. I had learned to seek the middle space between myself and the other, and to rest silently within this hallowed ground until the presence of Christ is felt. This presence comes "out of the blue" as insight that births entirely new possibilities. It descends as wisdom from above, revealing a vertically derived truth that is specifically perfect for any given situation—for healing manifests when the guidance sounding from angelic realms is clothed in words.

In the nine years I spent working with priests who practiced pastoral counseling out of an anthroposophical worldview, I gained invaluable insights into how the adversaries work in both individual and collective psychic fields. Later, when working with spiritually oriented medical doctors during my four-year therapeutic education training, my healing lens was further enhanced. Yet, nothing had prepared me to stand before a case where a precious human life was so clearly at stake. It would have been a relief to John's parents to just give him pharmaceuticals. Everyone could then be freed from having to muster the compassionate courage necessary to walk the thin line that John was going to be walking: between the magnetism of darkness and the hope of recovery. Choosing the path of relationship is a much deeper and longer commitment—one that bears the potential, moreover, of engendering a true and complete healing. The opposite of *dissociation* is *association*, which necessitates relationship.

Before I began this journey, I consulted with a colleague. I called Melissa, a doctor who advises me in my extreme therapeutic cases, making it as plain as can be that I did not know how to move forward and that I was not trained to deal with multiple personalities. There was a silence on the other end of the phone: "Melissa, are you there?" "Claudia," she said, "no one is trained to meet this! There are no rules, there is only the relationship. If you have that, you can find your way forward." And so we did.

John and I worked together for three years. There were three additional personalities that vied for dominance over his consciousness. One in particular was a very dark being, Leprus, who was a master of occult sciences. As John is a very intelligent person, it was not surprising that extremely intelligent subpersonalities would form. Another personality was Peter, who was oppositional, rude, aggressive, and combative. Then there was Zeleous, one who liked to walk the edge and foretell potential doom around each and every corner, warning of apocalyptic events ready to ambush John in each and every moment of time. John himself was conflict-avoidant, repressed, and committed to being the "good guy."

For months I battled with Leprus, outthinking him and thereby diminishing his occult control over John. I saw him as a sinister being that had entered into the abyss of separation in John's torn psyche, operating as a force of possession. The other two, Peter and Zeleous, I saw as healthy aspects of John's psyche which, due to his dissociation, were temporally problematic as they presented themselves as separate and autonomous entities. It was frustrating to John that I would never acknowledge Peter and Zeleous as individuals, friends, indwelling John as aliens to his natural self. I, however, never wavered on this score. He knew I had compassion for his experience of the autonomous beings inhabiting him, but that I actually loved the others too, as I saw them as part of his psychic wholeness.

Peter, in particular, would come into sessions with an enormous chip on his shoulder. He would try out his rudeness. I would address Peter directly, with uncompromising authority, informing him of how John would not take kindly to his being rude to me. My job was to love Peter and meet his combativeness with love. The same applied to the doom-saying Zeleous. But Leprus had to go. This dark being could have actually won over the individuality of John, resulting in a full-spectrum possession that would indeed have lured him over the edge, plunging him from the pinnacle of his consciousness—and leaving little hope that he would be able to return.

During Christmastide at the close of our first year together, Leprus was exorcised. This marked a magnificent achievement for John, who had convinced his remaining friends (Peter and Zeleous) that Leprus was evil and that banishing him would not destroy them, as Leprus had ominously warned them. After another two years, John went off to college, having accepted the fact that the other two were indeed aspects of himself, each irreplaceable for the integration he was seeking. He was finally ready to believe that he could mend the divide that was obstructing coherence. After leaving for college, he would come to see me during Christmas and summer breaks, each time sharing his continued success. Finally, I stopped hearing from him. Then I knew he had completed his work. He was whole.

The path John took was the hardest of all paths; and not only for John, but also for all those who walked it with him. Three years is a very long time to live with someone's psychic battle. It took enormous courage on his parents' part to go this long distance with their son while keeping faithful to the integral person that they believed would eventually emerge. The darkest of the three years was when satanic philosophies became a favorite. We held our ground, for we again had to outfox the devil.

There were no promises of success to lean into. His parents and I had to envision his wholeness with such constancy that we were able, finally, to overcome the "thought form" that the diagnosis of *dissociation* conjures, along with the drug treatments that typically accompany it. Every ounce of consciousness human beings had ever deposited in the "grid of dis-ease" has served to increase the power of "suggestion" that diagnosis can exert over a soul's inherent freedom. Against this, we had to triumph. In John's case, on the other hand, every ounce of consciousness we placed in the sphere of light increased his freedom from being sucked into the many mind traps that were seeking to destroy him.

Time is the great healer, yet its steady march has been stolen by interference patterns born of "constructed time." This time is human-made and is evident in high-speed technologies that whirl around us and through us in every second of our lives. Our relationship to Time is out of rhythm, resulting in a "hurried" pace that frenetically seeks immediate solutions in order to assuage the omnipresent state of anxiety that speed has engendered. We must take back time. If we can do this, we will remember the power of relationship and the cosmic rhythms of hours, days, seasons, and years. Time will again become a friend, in whose silence we will experience the "touch" of spiritual guidance that is eternally present. From this hallowed ground we will create a future of hope based on our faith in the power of love. The angels rejoice when this happens.

Meeting the Young Person Authentically

By Gabriel Cannon
in conversation with David Tresemer

DT: You work as a counselor with young people?

GC: To begin with, I use the term "mentor." By the time they come to me, many young people have had negative experiences with official "counselors" or "therapists."

DT: What kind of negative experiences are you talking about?

GC: Most of the young people I've met with have already been to some kind of "therapist," or several "therapists." Their experience was sitting in an office, face-to-face, with an adult whom they didn't know.... It felt very confrontational to them. Some of the young people will mock their previous therapist to me.

DT: Mock the therapists?

GC: Some of the stories are really funny. One of the young people said the session was like talking to someone on Skype and there's a delay in the video. They might say, "I would say something to him and he would just sort of sit there and look at me for a little while before kind of repeating back what I had just said to him, and it was this very awkward exchange."

DT: A blank stare and a pause.... Would you call that a misuse of Rogerian theory? [Carl Rogers was famous for defining "client-centered therapy," in which he recommended mirroring to the client what the client had said, so that the client could feel understood. While intended to include a warm restating of what the counselor had heard, some people made it mechanical, repeating back the words exactly, without warmth or understanding.]

GC: Yes, misuse of reflective listening—overly reflective.

DT: Overly reflective—you can polish the reflective mirror too much and you as counselor give back exactly what you gave, and you're not actually present for the client.

GC: I've used really basic reflective listening with young adults as well as adults. People older than adolescence actually appreciate exact reflection. But young people for some reason pick up on this technique really quickly and to them it feels like you're mocking them a little bit.

DT: Do you think that's because they're hypersensitive to feeling any technique being mechanically applied?

GC: I think so. I think adolescents in general are watching the therapist critically in a way that adults aren't. I think adults will come into the room, sit down, and immediately trust because they understand what therapy is. They dive right in. Adults are dying for someone to listen to them. They don't get that in their life and it feels so amazing that someone is simply listening, and can speak back what they had just said. For the client, it's all about them, and being heard.

Whereas young people are craving real relationship. They want someone to relate to them as an adult, as a person.

DT: Certainly we've been around young people who don't deserve adult status.

GC: Yes. They're growing in this area. The point is that young people are used to being talked at by their parents and teachers and not really listened to. Then they cross a threshold where then they want a different kind of relationship. A lot of the adults in their lives don't know how to make that transition. Parents still threaten them: "If you don't do your schoolwork, then you don't get to go to your friend's house!" Or reward them: "If you clean up your room, I'll give you some ice cream."

DT: For what age would those demands be appropriate?

GC: Children up to maybe eight, nine, ten.

DT: But the parents are using old methods...

GC: ...old methods. But the young people don't care about the ice cream anymore. The whole system of threat and reward hasn't kept up with them. For them, it's changed: "I actually want to have some agency in my life and I want to relate to you as if I'm a person; I want to be considered, my needs considered, and maybe this is how I like to keep my room, and I want you to understand why I keep my room this way, not tell me how to do it your way."

The other critique that young people have is discomfort in the therapeutic setting. They're sitting face-to-face, which creates tension. Traditional therapy gives you fifty minutes to do something. The therapist feels that pressure and can inadvertently pass that on to the client, and say in some way, subtle or overt, "We have to get to the issues, we have to accomplish something, and the clock is ticking."

DT: That's a version of fast, isn't it? We all know about "doorknob confessions" where the client has their hand on the doorknob as they're leaving the room and then comes the most important statement of the whole session. That should alert us to how time is messing with us. How do you deal with that?

GC: The majority of my clients are adolescent. I create a window in time that is flexible. Most therapists couldn't do this because it is quite difficult to schedule in this manner with many clients in one day. I usually tell my clients we have between an hour and a half to two hours to spend together, as much time as we need, and if we feel done being together at an hour and a half or even at an hour, then we can be done. If we're not done, we have two hours. Two hours is a long time. Rarely do I get to the point where we've been together for two hours and there still is a need to connect. A long window of time is one way to work with it and with that flexibility, and with them really knowing that they have this flexible window, they don't have to get right to the biggest issues.

That allows me to start very casually in the conversation, which is helpful for adolescents because they have to get warmed up to some of the deeper sharing. I start very casual, as you would check in with any person whom you haven't seen for a week: "Hey, how's it going, what's new in your life, what are you up to, how did that test go that we talked about last week?"—slowly getting into it. Within that conversation, that's where my counseling training will come in to sense the little access points. I can sense those things through their body language or tone or voice or some hesitancy. I look for those access points and note them. I don't dive right into an issue as soon as I see an opening. I note a little hesitancy when I ask, "How was your sister's visit—you haven't seen her in a while, and how was it?" I notice a little reluctance or they roll their eyes and try to evade by saying: "Well, I don't know, it was...whatever!" I notice maybe there's something there and I move on.

Once we feel warmed up, that's when I'll come back and say: "I really want to know more about your sister's visit; I want to hear what that was like for you." Then I can start to put a few little pressure points in there to try to open the situation up a little bit.

Also to reduce confrontation, I don't meet with adolescents in an office unless they want to, though they know that it's always an option.

DT: That's unusual. Where do you meet?

GC: For somebody working as a therapist for adolescents Monday through Friday, you've got 3:00 pm to 8:00 pm because they're in school all day. Most kids right after school, they have an after-school snack; most kids around 6:00 p.m. are having dinner. So we'll actually go get food together, which is a natural thing. We're sitting there having a slice of pizza or a burger or some sushi....

We'll have food, and we begin with casual conversation because it's usually not a very confidential place when we're sitting in a café or a pizza parlor. That's another reason I don't want to push and open too much in those moments. First share food together. Driving is such a great opportunity to connect with a young person because you're sitting side-by-side, you're not face-to-face, it doesn't feel as confrontational. Most therapists are legally not allowed to drive people in their car. I don't practice under the specific licensure that prohibits driving with a client, such as a licensed marriage and family therapist. However, as a mentor, I have more freedom to drive clients, to meet with them in public, things like that. With parental permission and the right car insurance, it's legal.

Another place we'll go sometimes is a park; we'll sit at a picnic bench. If I sit down and they sit next to me, then we sit side-to-side. They might sit down across from me, then we sit down across from each other.

DT: Do you sit down first on purpose?

GC: I try to sit down first…

DT: … to check them out, to see where…

GC: …where they want to sit. One of my most confidential outdoor settings is down by a creek where there's rushing water. I'll look for a place where there's a little waterfall creating an ambient loud noise where people passing by can't hear. This helps with confidentiality and the feeling for the client of confidentiality. There might be a clump of rocks. I'll sit down on a rock. Then they'll find their place and orient themselves to me how they would like to orient to me. It is usually side-by-side. I work mostly with adolescent males, so I think they prefer side-by-side. It feels more natural and less confrontational.

DT: How many of your clients have gone through Ritalin or any of the other drugs that are freely handed out now to young people, especially males? Have you encountered that? Are some of them still taking drugs of some kind?

GC: Yes, I have two sides of it. One is clients who are already diagnosed and on medication. And there are clients who have somebody in their life, often a teacher or some official at school, has told their parents that the young man fits this or that diagnosis, and now the parents are considering whether or not they should go the route of medication.

DT: That makes your role a very important one.

GC: It does, yes. I personally try not to hold a huge bias one way or the other. I try to be really open to both routes. My orientation is to hold off on a decision to medicate, and to look at other ways of treatment before using medication and, in certain circumstances, to consider coming off medication as an experiment. But I have to be careful with any advice in that regard. It's beyond my scope of competence to prescribe medication or to tell someone to stop taking it...

DT: ... to un-prescribe it ...

GC: Yes, I have to be really careful there. In my master's training, I was anti-medication. Then when I really worked with severe and persistent mental health issues, I saw some of the benefits of medications. I had to open my perspective. But with young people in particular, I think the problem with medication, and this was part of my thesis, was that many developmental issues in the adolescent stage of development look like adult disorders.

DT: That deserves repeating.

GC: Normal developmental issues within the adolescent years will look like adult mental health issues. An example is depression. Many adolescents quite normally turn inward: They're looking at themselves in a whole new way; they're not quite sure how they fit into the rest of the world or with their friend groups or in society; and they have depression-like symptoms. To me this is not "depression." It's actually "adolescence" that they are experiencing. They don't need antidepressants. They need someone who can help guide them through that specific passage of adolescence. Manic features also come out in adolescence, where they're exploring boundaries in a whole different kind of way ...

DT: ... staying up all night.

GC: Yeah, staying up, wanting to be on the phone all the time ...

DT: ... partying...the manic part. Do you think that that kind of behavior requires some kind of medication? A calming drug? Ritalin? Is that where alcohol fits in?

GC: Substance abuse is another example. Adolescents are experimenting with substances and shadow material of our culture; they're experimenting with drugs and alcohol; and that can look like adult substance abuse or addiction. But more accurately it's an experimental phase. It needs mentoring; it needs guidance; it needs someone to help them come into right relationship with those substances, because it's their first time doing it and sometimes they go a bit overboard.

DT: You seem to be saying that an adolescent has enough life forces to overdo a substance or behavior, but then bounce back, whereas an adult doesn't have the same degree of life force, and it's not part of their developmental program. The adults have settled down. If adults engage in that kind of behavior, they don't have the same ability to bounce back. It's not an experiment; it's more like a rut. Does that make sense?

GC: I like that way of describing it: The adults have dug themselves into a rut of familiarity, which can include pathological behavior. I think the same argument can be made around medications, that it would be probably worthwhile for the adolescent to experiment with other forms of treatment to get out of depression or alcoholism rather than jumping right toward medication as a treatment. I mean, that's where things like the DSM [*Diagnostic and Statistical Manual*, used by all agencies and therapists as the source of labels and numbers for a wide range of pathological syndromes] come in. The DSM is a tool that can be helpful I think for adults, but it's less applicable to adolescents.

DT: How does this relate to slow counseling?

GC: I think the relationship is of primary importance in therapy and in mentorship. Adolescents have to develop a certain amount of trust with the therapist, counselor, or mentor before they're really going to start to divulge any of their inner life, which for a lot of them they've never done with anyone.

To build that relationship takes time; it takes a slow approach. It takes doing some things that a lot of therapists don't do like meeting outside of an office. Self-disclosure is also important for an adolescent because adolescents tend, in my experience, not to really trust someone that they don't know anything about, someone who isn't revealing something important. If I'm not revealing some of my own life to them, then they may not reveal anything to me.

The rule in therapy is you can self-disclose if it serves the therapeutic process. It's part of the therapeutic process to build the relationship. I can say, "Oh, I have sisters too," or, "I also have a brother who's in jail." These can be little moments where they go, "Oh wow, you're a person too and you're having all these experiences and you've done some things in your life and I'm interested in that."

Sometimes part of the session is just them asking questions about me and I just freely give them answers.

DT: That then begins to change the client from an object into a person.

GC: Yeah, for the therapist.

DT: And for you too. That's one of the dangers for the therapist or counselor. In modern, fast therapy, the client becomes a treatment plan, and you give them, in some cases, twenty minutes a week, and a new diagnosis from the DSM. In that kind of factory approach, the client becomes an object—and the therapist becomes an object also. When you do that all day every day, it takes a toll.

GC: On the therapist, I agree. It takes time to get to know each other. I have some clients now who after four or five months of mentorship are, in their parents' perspective, doing better. They're more successful in school, they're more successful in the home relationships, they're doing better. Sometimes the parents speak, "Okay, they're all good now, they're all better." Some of those parents will end the mentoring process, which of course is their choice. I tell them to let me know if you need me in the future. What usually happens in a few weeks or months later, they'll call back and say, "Uh, something else has come up...."
Then I have to come in and in a way start over. We have to get to know each other again, because for an adolescent three months is a long time; they've gone through all kinds of changes in three months. If I step back in they have the attitude, "You don't really know me anymore." I've been encouraging parents to not suspend mentorship altogether, rather space it out more so that I meet with the client once a month, even for just a short forty-five minutes or an hour: "Let's go get some food and check in with each other... "

DT: ... because they've created a relationship with you and then it's been artificially terminated by their parents' pocketbook because the parents are looking at the kid as an object with symptoms. Perhaps the parents, in their fast-paced lives, don't understand actually what's happening deep down, that it's about the tending of a relationship. And you as counselor or mentor have to cope with the parents' process as well.

GC: I'm learning ways to do that, even ways where, if it is about money, I can gift a family thirty minutes a month. It's worth it for me in the long run to maintain some kind of connection, for the time when I come back in and work with that family when they need it. As a mentor for adolescents, I often end up working with the parents.

A principle of family systems work is that there's the identified patient, the IP. It's usually one of the kids who is acting out in some way. So the family goes into therapy saying, "We have to help that kid." The IP is the problem. But in a family systems perspective that kid is exhibiting symptoms as a way to bring the outside world's attention to dysfunction in the family system. I as counselor am the first connection between the family and the outside world.

I hold that perspective for the parents that call me because their kid is acting out or getting into trouble or doing bad things. I have to find a way to invite the parents: "Are you also open to changing the way that you parent?" One has to be very gentle with how one brings that up to parents because sometimes it's really clear that it is a mother or father that needs to learn how to work with their developing child, to learn that the young one is not a child anymore, that they're actually an adolescent, and a whole new system of rules has to come in.

Sometimes I do a family mediation, which is sitting down with the whole family. I act as an advocate for the IP, helping him or her say something to the parents, helping him or her to make really clear requests, and then helping him or her to redefine boundaries and styles of communication. That can be very challenging for parents to change in that way. But it's an important part of supporting that adolescent's growth—through the difficulties of that life stage, which may appear troublesome, but are quite normal.

DT: Helping the adolescent, and meanwhile assisting the parents' growth also.

GC: Yes.

Relationship as a Pathway to Growth

By Lila Sophia Tresemer

The promise of "happiness" in relationship has been alluring to couples since the beginning of time. The elusive nature of relational happiness is the subject of thousands of self-help books. Are there simple hints to discovering a pathway to relational joy? Is there an approach that can shift our expectations of relationship given how many relationships apparently "fail"?

Important note: Fail is not a word we personally use in regard to past relationships. Our sense of building a stronger basis for learning and growing is founded on the principle that we learn and grow from challenges in life, and relationships are the most reliable way for that learning to occur.

The word *relationship* has in it a genius. The prefix *re-* means bringing back, or coming back to. The *-lat-* comes from *latus*, meaning some thing you bear or carry. The next part, the suffix *-tion*, confers on the word a thingness, as in a state or condi-*tion* or ac-*tion*. You keep coming back to this thing, whatever it is, that you are bearing. The *-ship* part comes from the old Proto-Indo-European *skap*, meaning to create or ordain. You create or ordain or recognize a thing that has weight, a thing that exists within

every Two, and you keep
coming back to it. Some-
times you renew inten-
tion with the same part-
ner, and sometimes you
change partners to start
the whole process over
again. The word *relationship* collects reminders
about what relationships
are, and what their pos-
sibilities can be. Rudolf

Steiner said that the main thing we take with us when we
die is our relationships. We leave all the possessions behind;
relationship is the one "thing" that we carry past the threshold of death.

We created a visual play on the idea of the "ship" that car-
ries our "relating" in the first edition of what has now become
The Conscious Wedding Handbook (Sounds True, 2015).
The colorful sunset that illuminates our romantic notion
of happily-ever-after is often an illusion that may last for a
couple years, before the more demanding work of relationship demands our attention. Pretty picture gone, and time for
the work of relationship. Can we reframe the promise of fairy
tale marriages, without losing the sun and sea and jumping
dolphins? Can we find some deeper meaning in the pursuit of
long-term relationship, by approaching it with more realistic
expectations and sophisticated understanding of the underlying issues of "soul"? Psyche traditionally meant soul, thus psychology was the patterns of the soul: Can we find the soul connection to self and other, and ride that "ship" into new places?

Our research and practical suggestions are reported in our book, *The Conscious Wedding Handbook*. But here we can summarize some of that research and take it a bit further.

From our work with couples over decades, we have concluded that one important shift can result from reframing some beliefs and expectations. A key myth-busting is summed up in the phrase "Relationship is not for happiness."

A look at the various shipwrecks in the waters of anyone's life would support that idea. There they lie, recognizable by shape and size, wrecked but oddly not rotting. Surely they should be returning their structures to basic components— iron and other minerals—that can be used in future constructions? What pain are you holding onto that keeps these wrecks from dissolving?

Were these past attempts at relating all failures? No...most likely the lessons learned from relating can be applied to future understanding and insight. But the context of the cultural belief of "happily-ever-after" needs to be reconsidered, and different values put in its place. You can come to understand that relationship is not for happiness, and replace the formula with one more authentically realistic:

> *Relationship is a living process through which*
> *each person becomes a better human being.*

A committed, conscious, living relationship will cause you and your partner to develop, to mature, to grow, and to blossom. The process may include experiences that are painful. Your partner becomes partly your live-in therapist, who will learn about your secrets and your irksome habits and will—either gently or with exasperation— cause you to look at yourself, and perhaps—yes, we should say it—cause you to *change*. You will *change*. We didn't say you *may* change—we said you *will* change. Relationships, ideally, are all about lifting the veils of illusion to rediscover truth. Our culture has many notions of relationship that can create illusions between you. You put on the rose-colored glasses and your partner sure does look rosy. Some think that working on relationship means finding ways to maintain the illusion of happiness. We don't approach relationship that way, and haven't seen any couples who can successfully fool themselves for very long. If you connect to your soul and to the soul of the other, the veils will lift and something extraordinary happens. There before you stands a living, breathing, life-filled inspiration of soul. You see it in the other, and you see it in yourself. The question is how to accomplish that. How do you lift the veils and become authentic with one another, deliberately and by choice? Communication tools are a good place to begin. Taking the time to sit together with some basic agreements to deeply listen and learn from one another is a first step.

We strongly recommend a Heart Talk technique, which involves a few simple ground rules, to which both people must agree in order to build a safe container.

1. Choose an item to hold; it can be a crystal, a special stick, or anything easily held in your hand. Whoever has the talking piece speaks. The other one does not speak.

2. The person listening is attentive and interested, not planning what to say next. *Do not interrupt* one another, not even for clarifications, as these apparently innocent interruptions often have emotional tone attached. Not interrupting is key and must be honored or the field of trust won't be created. If an interruption does occur (some habits are challenged by

change), simply reaffirm the agreements and start again. As you listen, you may feel tempted to prepare a rebuttal. However, let your prepared comments drift away. You don't have to respond to every single thing that was said. Let yourself listen, rather than prepare, and what comes out of you when it's your turn will be more genuine.

3. Once you're finished speaking, *lay the talking piece down.* Don't hand it to the other person. This allows for silence and relaxation in the communication. The other person will pick it up when he or she is ready to respond. Silence and deep breathing are part of this process, and something we don't often experience in normal conversations.

4. Be as concise as possible in speaking, and don't go on too long or change subjects too quickly. Express one thought. Allow it to sink in. Then lay the talking piece down to give your partner the opportunity to respond. More important than you emptying yourself of all you have to say is that you are heard in what you do say. So don't say too much.

5. Don't use this as an opportunity to "dump" energetically or verbally. As much as possible, speak in "I" statements, rather than blaming or accusatory statements. Say, "I feel hurt by the way the communication happened." This opens up things more than saying, "You hurt me in the way you communicated." Speak from your own feelings and experience. If you're the one who feels hurt, that's not the other's fault— these are your feelings, right?

6. Be respectful of one another, no matter how difficult the area of communication might be. Remember, this is your Beloved across from you in this process.

7. As much as possible, take one hundred percent responsibility for creating your experience, reaction, or response to

RELATION-SHIP-WRECKS

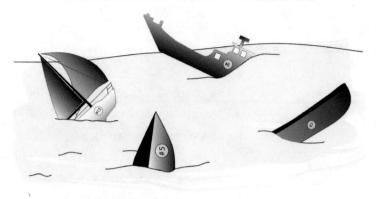

whatever is said in the Heart Talk. This might be a new concept to some—watch closely and you'll see how challenging it can be.

8. Let the conclusion of the Heart Talk be decided by both parties, and then conscientiously lay down the talking piece and allow the communication to return to easy conversation. Try not to end prematurely, as often breakthroughs happen as a result of perseverance.

You have the potential, with the help of your partner, for learning what true Love is, a Love that will change the way you think and feel about everything in the world, making everything more potent and delicious, a Love that fires you in each morning's dawn to engage with the world and everyone in it, a Love that acquaints you with angels. This is latent in everyone; it can become your experience.

Those who have been in relationship a long time know that human beings aren't given at birth the tools to make a relationship work. They are given an impetus—sexual attraction or the mystery of Love—that draws them together. But most people don't know what to do after that. You have to learn

the skills to make the relation-ship endure, grow, and teach you what it can about yourself. This takes extraordinary vulnerabil-ity. It takes openness to bubble-busting. It takes intention, choice, and work. And the rewards for growing in true Love are well worth the effort. They will, in fact, lead to an oceanic swell of deep wellbeing, and, eventually, to true joy. As illustrated, the old relation-ship-wrecks slowly dissolve into the sea, giving you back the energy that you've tied up in them. The lessons from previous relationships are bet-ter integrated into a calm sea of Spirit Knowing.

A Drinking Problem

By David Tresemer

Part 1: Climbing the Ladder

"I had no choice: I had to have a drink."
"What were you drinking?"
"Wine—I only drink wine. I proceeded to drink a whole bottle, gulp...by...gulp."
This last statement was made with a tone of bitterness. He winced with the pain of each recollected gulp....

In the therapeutic encounter, every word and every nuance has to be observed—and more than observed: The therapist participates in every word and nuance. In this short exchange lay hints as to the "problem" as well as to the "cure," two terms that we have come to associate with psychology—labels that are as dangerous as the binge drinking itself.

The sense of "no choice" marks the experience of addiction. The person feels helpless, yet acts. We all have those moments—after a large Thanksgiving dinner, "I can't believe I ate the whole thing!" We can have the experience of waking up the next day or even later on during a party wondering "who is in charge of my body?" We can also have the uncanny experience of observing ourselves do something that we don't want to do at the moment that we are doing it. That's actually more awake, though more painful. I noted that my client was able to do that.

Because of showing up to work repeatedly with a hangover (at this point, he was not drinking during the day), the client planned to visit a psychologist. Sometimes, the workplace requires the employee to consult a psychologist. In either case, the visit to the psychologist is often thought of as the "last resort," the least preferred option.

Why is that? Why are psychologists sometimes feared? "You're a psychologist?—Have you analyzed me yet? Do you know what I'm thinking?" The client's caution alerts us that the symptom is serving a function, and that function does not wish to be seen or changed.

A large proportion of mainstream psychology perceives the symptom as the problem. If you can get rid of the symptom, then you have a happier worker—no hangovers in the mornings, more hours during the day to lead a productive life. To the therapist working out of transpersonal and anthroposophic psychology, the symptom is a pointer. It takes time to figure out to what it's pointing, but a pointer it certainly is— toward a deeper issue, toward a block to soul growth, toward an abyss that the person has to leap in his or her journey, and sometimes toward a secret treasure necessary to move forward.

With this client it became clear after a few sessions that there was an intense desire for an experience beyond the daily/ usual/mundane. Alcohol seemed an easy route. Indeed, alcohol has been used in many societies through time as a quick high—through "spirits" to the spiritual. But alcohol lifts you quickly to the third floor of a massive edifice, high but no way to go higher. You scratch the walls trying to find a way to lift

to a more refined and powerful experience. To go beyond the
third floor, to the more powerful, to the more refined, you
have to go back down to the ground floor, enduring the "low"
that this descent brings, and then climb a ladder that takes
you as far up as you would like. To go down, to recover, and
then to climb each rung of the ladder requires that the out-of-
control will forces be reined in—that the "no choice" voiced
in the first admission of my client becomes a choice. There's
a hint in what was said: "no choice" was followed by "I only
drink wine." It may be a false rationalization, but it is the
beginning of thinking through a subject, and applying it to
the direction of will, to a sense of choice that can, through
counseling, become stronger and stronger. We have to listen
carefully to every word, for upon them an approach is made
to assisting the client to rediscover the soul's path.

What has been accomplished with this client is a good first
step. What are the other dynamics, such as the challenge of
self-hatred that often comes with substance abuse? How does
the therapist actually help? These questions await a future
column....

PART 2: WHY DRINK?

In the first part, we listened in on a brief exchange with a
person with a "drinking problem." What about that word,
"problem"? Originally meaning "something thrown forward,"
as in a geometry "problem," it has come to mean something
difficult—something thrown into your way or "in your face."
When a drinking problem comes into the office, it can earn
from the *Diagnostic & Statistical Manual* (DSM, version
5) a formal name and a number—in this example, Alcohol
Use Disorder F10.10, or if more severe F10.20. If you can get

yourself another diagnosis—such as Depression (various numbers for that syndrome)—you are on the road to getting support from your employer's insurance carrier.

The dominant psychological method in clinics and VA hospitals is presently Cognitive Behavioral Therapy (CBT), wherein the therapist and client catalogue the problem behaviors and then devise a stepwise approach to changing the client's thought patterns—the cognitive part—and thereby changing the behavior. The success of this method in ceasing those symptoms has been supported by several studies. And yet the alcoholics are a tough group. They tend to slip back after the treatment.

Dr. Roberta Nelson, Faculty Chair for the Anthroposophic Psychology course, and in the trenches at a residential treatment center in North Dakota, always asks a client with a drinking problem, "What benefit does drinking give you?" She has observed that this question is never asked by mainstream psychologists. An anthroposophic approach insists on asking this question.

Drinking alcohol shows an underlying desire to find spirit—through "spirits." The drinker seeks the alteration of time and space, the wobble in perceptions, the giddiness, the feeling of abandon with the promise of getting ever "higher".... The drinker is looking for something beyond the mundane, and then gets caught in the quest. Some report that the word itself comes from the Arabic *al-ghawl*, "the demon," source of the English word "ghoul." *Al-ghawl* is also source of the name of the star Algol, the Eye of Medusa that turns you to stone; perhaps this relates to one epithet for drunkenness: "stoned." Spirits in alcohol were known from early days, yet not a helpful kind of spirit. The spirits raise you up, and then crash you down. Thus the question that Dr. Nelson asks becomes, "What are you seeking?" In its practical emphasis only on behavior, CBT bypasses this question of motivation.

The responses to Dr. Nelson's question at first detail the feelings of being lifted up and then crashed to the ground. Then the clients describe brief glimpses of something important seeking them. Swirled about by the demons that they have invoked to aid them in meeting this something, they hold on to that hope. They feel, "Maybe next time I will get there."

An anthroposophic psychologist has a framework gleaned and integrated from the far-flung and relatively disorganized references from Rudolf Steiner, and developed through the anthroposophic psychologist's own life experience and inner work. Thus, when the anthroposophic psychologist affirms the existence of that which the client seeks—soul and spirit, who also are seeking the client—it comes from the confidence of personal experience. In effect, the anthroposophic psychologist says, "What you are seeking is real. It is personal; it is intimate; it requires discipline to find and maintain contact. It will be with you always, and is seeking to relate to you. You may not realize what you correctly intuited until you've cleaned up, as alcohol won't take you there. Cleaning up may take you further away from what you feel is the call of your soul. You have to go back downstairs, even into the basement, before you can find a better way up, down past where you were stuck with the alcohol; then you can go further up, without obstruction."

Does the therapist say these words? Not likely, as they may not relate to the everyday struggles of the client. These words are held inwardly and known as true by the anthroposophic psychologist. The client I began with ceased drinking, then was pressured by his buddies, "Aw, c'mon; it's Jake's birthday! One drink won't hurt you!" One drink became several. This put him back many steps. These are the pressing issues that come into the therapist's room; in that circumstance the words in the paragraph above may appear as merely pleasant homilies.

One wonders about my client's buddies: What motivated them to ensnare their friend into the substance again? It helps to posit the existence of adversarial forces or retarding forces, and we can approach this in the next column.

Part 3: It wasn't me . . .

"I can't believe that it was me doing those things. Nah, it wasn't me. It couldn't have been me."

We've been following a client who came in because of excessive use of alcohol, and looking at the distinctive approach of anthroposophic psychology. In this column, we consider the very challenging subject: "it wasn't me." Challenging because mainstream psychology assigns all behavior to the actor, and returns the verdict, "Yes, it was you—that darkness is part of you." They deliver this verdict either with a stern reprimand, leading to blame and punishment through the agency of the law, or with a compassionate offer to help transform the unacceptable behavior.

In the instance of my client, the unacceptable behavior included shouting, cursing, calling others vile names, making up stories, pushing, and, on one occasion, ganging up on one of their drinking buddies to pull his shirt off and douse him with beer. In that place, late at night, brawls occurred around him, though he never was in one. The repeated experience of his crushing remorse on the day after compelled him to come in to speak with me.

When he said the words at the beginning of this piece, shaking his head slowly from side to side, staring off to the distance down to his left, he was reliving primarily the anxiety of not knowing who or what he was, deep down, in full truth. The mystery of what lay down there was for him a Pandora's box full of horrors. He wanted to close the lid. And yet he still had this compulsion to go drinking....

Sigmund Freud spoke and wrote of the "subconscious" and "unconscious" in the human being. He saw lurking in those depths "primal processes" and urges to aggression, domination, rage, murder. He sought to expose these contents to the light of consciousness, thus to integrate them into the whole personality. Carl Jung, Freud's student, began to crack this open a bit further—human beings are like islands poking up out of the ocean: In the darkness beneath the ocean's surface, all the islands are connected with each other and with grander realities, not only to aggression but also to cosmic splendors.

Anthroposophic psychology goes another step. Though the figures of Satan and Devil have been rejected by modern science, Rudolf Steiner reintroduced them for us to understand ourselves and the plight of our fellow human beings. Steiner spoke at length about these as two different forces, and used the names Ahriman for Satan, and Lucifer for the Devil. Briefly, Ahriman, the name of the anti-life-force from Persian lore, promotes hatred, coldness, hardness of intellect, and rejection of anything spiritual. Lucifer, a Latin name meaning light bearer, promotes fantastical escapes from reality: Lucy in the sky with diamonds. I call them the Hardener and the Illusionist. One of their greatest strengths comes from the fact that most people have been trained to think that they don't exist.

Steiner was very careful with these concepts, as premature assignment of one's thoughts, feelings, or deeds to retarding spirits—"The Devil made me do it"—can land you in a pile of confusion. Blaming demons has led to the excesses of the Inquisition and modern fundamentalist groups.

Experiencing invisible independent entities outside yourself can land you in several diagnostic categories from the *Diagnostic & Statistical Manual* (DSM-5), ranging from Schizo-Typal personality disorders to full-blown schizophrenia, and others. Anthroposophic psychologists risk these diagnoses daily. However, though misuse of these perceptions of spirits can be dangerous, they are extremely helpful. One observes where the gaps or vulnerabilities of the personality permit entry of negative influences. Anthroposophy as a philosophy gives a thorough conceptual framework for understanding the Hardener and the Illusionist, with, however, little practical guidance for recognizing their presence and knowing how to deal with them. That's the work of the anthroposophic psychologist.

Working with the client, I could slowly build the case for how drinking opened up certain psychic vulnerable places, first for the Illusionist—the celebration part of the evening, full of camaraderie and laughter and attraction, floating up above the pain of the day—and then for the Hardener—the place where aggression and hatred appeared, then turned against oneself and against others, where the ugly and nasty rose up, where paranoia led to lashing out. When you have the client on-side and observing these phenomena with you, you can identify those vulnerable places, and begin the process of sealing them against intruders, while opening the heart to true relationships.

PART 4: CONSCIENCE

We have been following a man with a drinking problem, seen through the eyes of anthroposophic psychology.

What is the worst part of the experience? The suffering of the hangover? The loss of faculties? The loss of time even to the extent of arrested development? The impacts on family and friends?

Unless the drinker has seriously harmed another, the most severe cost experienced by the drinker is the withering condemnation of self-judgment, the annihilating cold wind of guilt, the hatred of one's own existence. It's enough to "drive one to drink"—and that is the typical method used to avoid these punishments. However, in order to maintain life, the body repeatedly rejects the poisons forced upon it: Drinking fails as an escape.

To assist someone through this negative cycle, the psychologist must distinguish between the different forms of conscience.

Children mimic the patterns of their parents. They learn by interjecting ways of doing things, along with ways of feeling and thinking. One group of patterns was termed by Sigmund Freud the "superego," a function over and above (super) the executive function of the personality (ego). If a two-year-old approaches a hot woodstove, the parent shouts, "Don't touch! Hot!" The shock of the shout can send the child into a crying fit even without touching the stove. In a way, the parent has substituted one trauma for another, with the reasoning that the shouting is better than a burn. Dozens of these experiences create a pattern in the psyche of the child, what some call a "parent introject." As children by their nature seek to learn everything possible about their environment, there is a constant stream of evaluations of "good, that worked" and "oops, that didn't work." For most people, that latter evaluation has been given an overlay of "bad." From the woodstove incident, the child internalizes the commanding voice, "Stop!," and often the commanding voice, "Bad boy!" The mighty parent thus exercises his or her god-like power to the child by blasting him. Though parent effectiveness training can assist adults to train (both children and pets) more efficiently, the imprint is still made.

The superego harbors a collection of rules-of-thumb on how to stay safe, as well as devastating rejections. When the client confronts this introject, he experiences it as worse than death—it threatens complete annihilation. You can observe this in bar fights, struggles at the edges of "bad."

Now for the other side of conscience, the part not recognized by mainstream psychology, that is so very useful to the anthroposophic psychologist.

The picture is this: Conscience is the work of angels who show you the consequences of your actions, even as you are considering them, or when they are impulses not yet realized!

You can verify this in your own experience by examining the split seconds between an impulse and an action. In the case of drinking, you pay attention to the few moments after you feel the urge to walk to the cupboard and pull out a bottle of something, or the few moments that you imagine a cool spiked drink of some kind. What happens in those moments?

There appears to me a unique breed of archangels who specialize in offering these reflections to human beings. The clearer the view into the future of how your (potential) actions ripple out in every direction affecting you and all those around you, the better. These archangels work with your personal angel to help you understand and thus found a decision based on the facts of the matter, that is, on how your dharma affects your karma. There are occasions where even more potent angelic beings are called into action. The story of Dorian Gray examines this notion of reflection of consequences. The misdeeds and crimes of Dorian Gray did not appear on his physiognomy, but in a portrait of him kept hidden in his closet. (This is illustrated in the brilliant painting by Ivan Albright at the Art Institute of Chicago, well worth a visit to see, as the online version misses much of the detail.) The consequences land somewhere, and the conscience pictures this to our souls on a regular basis.

When you open to that level of knowing, you then begin to realize that there are also beings of great power who wish to befuddle you and guide you to actions with negative consequences. They seek to dull or smear the reflections offered by the reflecting (arch)angels.

Conscience is the great battleground of the human soul. Here is where human beings rise or fall in their long-term soul development, both individually and as a group with purpose.

An approach based on anthroposophic psychology distinguishes between the practical superego, the punishing superego, and true conscience. When we engage in "whole-soul conversation" with another, it leaves room for the soul to come forward, to step through the rubble of self-recriminations, and begin to see a larger picture. Conscience can then work in one's favor, helping one see the constructive consequences of rebuilding. Then begins the longer term work of restoration—permitting the memories to arise, one by one, and negotiating the forgiveness necessary for each and every deed of the past. This process can help with the temptations of the present—the temptation to have another drink.

Part 5: Perception of Time and Expansiveness of Perception

A treatment plan for someone with a drinking problem can include training the client to learn how to stretch time. We need this skill for many areas of our lives. If, for example, you seek to enter inner worlds through meditation, you have to learn to stretch the time between waking and sleeping, between consciousness and no-consciousness. You have to learn the characteristics of the small gap between waking and sleeping, and then stretch time to open that gap further.

The alcoholic must learn to stretch time, to slow down the important moments between the urge and the action, between feeling the desire and the pulling the bottle out of the cupboard. To develop the faculty of slowing time and observing oneself requires repeated attempts. You must observe on many occasions the body acting in a way that the mind regrets, then endure the loss of focus induced by the drug, knowing that you'll have a new opportunity tomorrow.

The more you stretch time, the more you perceive the hundred negotiations at every movement. You begin to experience the influences of others and even to hear voices.

In the previous column I named the superego as the loudest internal voice. Its judgmental proclamations stay loud, even though you may try to drown them out. Though loudest, they are not the most powerful.

Most powerful are the archangels who specialize in mirroring to you the consequences of your actions. Working with your best or higher self, these comprise your conscience.

In between the superego and the angels lie a large variety of beings who are "across the threshold" that separates the seen and the unseen, that separates the physical and the energetic—that separates the living and the so-called dead.

Rudolf Steiner is unique amongst philosophers in his emphasis on the so-called dead. (I have brought together much of what he had to say about it in a paper, "The Importance of the So-Called Dead," that I have put in the Research section of the www.StarWisdom.org website.) He has even said that the proper evolution of humanity depends on increasing our communication with the so-called dead. Steiner observes the dead working through us all the time, especially through our faculties of feeling and willing (doing), and sometimes through our thinking. That is how we can come to know their activity, by observing our own feelings, deeds, and thoughts.

I emphasize "so-called" because Steiner suggested that these beings are not dead but living, though in a different form. As always, the difference between "Steiner says" and true Anthroposophy lies in verification through personal experience. Steiner points the way but, unless you confirm these indications, they remain mere concepts.

The notion of life after death and what happens then has had an increasing number of promoters and detractors. Things changed when the physician Eben Alexander had a Near-Death Experience (NDE) and wrote about it. Now he's giving talks at conferences, and the whole issue has received new attention. The materialists persist in explaining these experiences as chemical aberrations. Perhaps the duality between materialists and spiritualists will never end. Again, it depends on your experience and what you discover by stretching time (though some materialists also reject personal experience, leaving ... what?).

Here is the special relationship with alcohol. While all of us have regular access to those over the threshold of spirit, and filter out much that comes to and through us, alcohol has a loosening effect on those discernments. In other words, alcoholics have many more of the dead, and many more of lower quality, working through them. With the ability to stretch time, one can begin to observe them.

At every juncture, you can observe one or more "spirits" or "influences" working with you. As the mind—thinking—observes the body go to the bookshelf, reach in behind a certain book to a hiding place, pull out a bottle, unscrew the top, take a swig, screw the top back on, pause, unscrew it and take another swig, put the bottle back, rearrange the books, go to the bathroom, swish the mouth with water so no one will notice booze on the breath.... As you open up each of these movements to careful observation, you begin to feel and sometimes perceive others working through you. Then you can begin to formulate your side of the conversation, your choices of which spirits over the threshold with whom you would prefer to commune.

This is a process that benefits from the guidance of an anthroposophic psychologist.

Part 6: Sweetness—its Attractions and Dangers

We have followed a client beset by a drinking problem. Here we will finish the inquiry, looking at a few other issues that I haven't emphasized before.

Let's start with sugar. Some people say that alcohol metabolizes to sugar, and this hyperglycemia is the cause of the hangover, the addiction, and so forth. Actually alcohol does not metabolize to sugar, but rather to acetaldehyde, a very toxic substance and known carcinogen. Before it breaks down to acetate, that toxin can wreak havoc in the liver.

So it seems that sugar is let off the hook. Not really. My client is not rare in his preference for stout, sherry, and mixed drinks that all complement the alcohol with heavy doses of sugar. Some of these drinks have a full daily supply of sugar—9 teaspoons for men and 6 teaspoons for women, as recommended by the American Heart Association—in two drinks. After that, it promotes what the experts call "de novo lipogenesis," meaning new fat formation, as well as serious problems with insulin production, leading over time toward "metabolic syndrome" and a higher risk of heart disease, diabetes, and stroke.

I had wondered for years what is so attractive about sweetness? The nutritionist John Yudkin helped me when he explained that high sweetness in fruits and vegetables is a reliable indicator of maximum yield of vitamins, minerals, and phytonutrients. By sweetness we measure the value of a food (and perhaps a relationship as well...read on). Sugar is important in itself as a nutrient but those other items are harder to find. The problem is that modern science has stripped the indicator of sweetness—sugar—away from what it was indicating—nutrition.

An important observation about sweetness comes from insights of Rudolf Steiner and Ita Wegman, who worked on an approach to medicine based on Anthroposophy. In *Fundamentals of Therapy*, they distinguish between the various bodies of the human being—the physical substance body, the etheric or vital body, the astral body full of thoughts and feelings, and the "I." The "I" is the individuality, mostly in spirit realms though it interpenetrates the other bodies. Steiner and Wegman write about how different substances— plants or minerals or essences of either—work into the various bodies. For sugar, they say that it interacts directly with the "I," fosters the "I," brings it more into prominence in relation to the other bodies.

Can you now make sense of your joy at the enjoyment of a ripe peach, juice dripping down your chin? Can you make sense of the increased consumption of sugar in the Western world, as an indicator of thirst for the "I"? Perhaps here is an answer for "Why do you use artificial sweeteners?" The usual argument is that they lead to less "de novo lipogenesis," though they can confuse the insulin system and, as with aspartame, act as toxins. The answer to the question, "Why?," is "Because I am seeking the Spirit."

In another place, Steiner implies the same about alcohol. This makes a mixed drink of sugar and alcohol, such as a margarita or a piña colada or a Mai Tai, or sherry or stout, into a quick road to Spirit. A phrase from Theosophy, "storming the gates of heaven," pertains here. The consumer of alcohol and its frequent companion sugar charges forward, piling spirits on spirits, to get to Spirit.

That underlying yearning for Spirit has to be understood in any conversation with an alcoholic. Thus the "I am"

statement used in groups for those with a drinking problem—"Hello, my name is Fred; I am an alcoholic."—limits
the identity of the drinker to the habit, not to the longing. A
more accurate statement might be: "Hello, my name is Fred; I
am an embodied soul yearning to experience the Spirit foundation of my existence." The eagerness for Spirit drives the
behavior. If Spirit is really the aim—and with my client, this
became increasingly clear—then is drinking the best method
to achieve it? As the hangovers get worse, as the liver scari-
fies (the slow process of cirrhosis), as the overwhelmed liver
dumps toxins into the blood stream, as the "I" retreats further and further from one's experience, one would think that
the client would understand that this method isn't working.
But by this time, the insulin system may be wrecked, and the
pain may be so great that one craves the one known effective
panacea, more drink. Going back down to the ground floor
may take months or years, before a healthier approach to
Spirit can be discovered.

As the main locus for metabolism of alcohol is the liver,
one can ask if Jupiter—the planet that rules the liver—is
involved. In the case of my client, there was a square (right
angle) between Jupiter and Pluto at birth, meaning a tension and a drawing of the influence of Jupiter into Pluto's
underworld. In that case, one looks for other relations to the
planet Jupiter, either at birth or from a planet passing over
those positions, as opportunities to ameliorate the negative
expression of this right angle (square). In the case of my client, this involved a trine (the "sweet" aspect) between Venus
and Jupiter at birth. When Venus moving in the sky ("tran-
siting") came directly over the birth–Venus position, I was
on the lookout for a new relationship in my client's life. It

came, a chance meeting, seemingly insignificant, though he thought "there might be something there." I suggested that he find out more. She has since then become a very positive and stabilizing influence in his long road of recovery. With alcoholism, as with any dependence or habit pattern, the main work is to build the small-s self, the basic functioning part of the human being that permits one to live in the world, into a large-S Self. This involves all the bodies, physical, etheric, and astral, in order to create a safer container for the "I," the Spirit that one seeks through spirits. A sweet relationship—in his case, a living Venus—can assist.*

---

* This article first appeared as a series of columns in *Lilipoh* magazine.

Slowly Following the Leads

By Jennifer Stickley

When I was around fifteen years old, I decided that I was going to learn how to meditate. I am not even sure how I came to this decision. I had no family members or friends who meditated. Maybe we talked about it in my high school world religions class? Maybe I read a novel based in the 1960s that mentioned it? All I can remember now, at 42, was being in my bedroom and opening the book that I had checked out from the county library, entitled something along the lines of "How to Meditate," and following the instructions: "Sit quietly, and focus on your breathing...."

Almost immediately, I found myself in a place that was so vast, so very huge...and yet at the same time I felt so small, tiny, as though I was completely dissolving away. I remember thinking, "Wow, I am smaller than an atom," and the very next thought, the nail in the coffin, so to speak, "I wonder if this is what it's like to die?" With that thought, I was struck with pure panic in my heart. I opened my eyes, and quickly shut the book on meditation for well over 20 years.

When my son was six, we moved from Florida to Oregon. My husband had just gotten a job as a professor of Chinese medicine. We had been invited to a party and I didn't know anyone there. My son started chatting with a man in the living room by asking, "Do you know about Ganesha?" The man answered "Why yes, I do." I listened in while they chatted intently about many deities and, as we were leaving to go, I said to my husband, "I don't know what it is, but I just love that guy who was talking to our son." My husband responded, "you should go have tea with him sometime." What I came to find out was that this man is a tea collector and considered himself a "tea monk." He had lived in an ashram for many years and was now offering classes on the energetics of teas. I spent every Saturday morning of the following year attending a tea and meditation class. With the help of the relaxing and energetically opening teas, I learned to soften my gaze in order to see more sharply and more clearly. Colors became more brilliant, the shadows became just as present as the light, the rose's petal formation more intricate. I learned to feel comfortable and safe with my energy expanding and contracting. With the guidance and counsel of someone who had spent many years practicing meditation, I was able to let go of my fear of meditation and began living in a more mindful and engaged way with the world around me. During this time of tea and meditation, I deepened my practice of feng shui, decided to study herbalism, and later the art of counseling. It has been a slow process, learning to follow the leads with curiosity, one that could not have been rushed, one that unfolded in its own time.

(The artwork by Benjamin König and the poem were found and recommended by Jennifer Stickley to go together, in the spirit of her following the leads, following the seeds....)

Starmoney *by Benjamin König*

The Soul's Longings Are like Seeds
by Rudolf Steiner

The soul's longings are like seeds,
Out of which deeds of will are growing
And life's fruits are ripening.
I can feel my destiny and my destiny finds me.
I can feel my star and my star finds me.
I can feel my aims and my aims are finding me.
The World and my soul are one great unity.
Life grows brighter around me
Life becomes harder for me
Life will be richer within me.

The Art of Living:
Slow Counseling and Art Converge

By Micheal Hooker

"The line between art and life should be kept as fluid, and perhaps as indistinct, as possible." — Allan Kaprow

In 2015, the Association for Anthroposophic Psychology (AAP) launched a three-year certificate program in Anthroposophic Counseling Psychology in upstate New York. Having a background in somatic and transpersonal therapies, I welcomed the opportunity to explore this new beau ideal of slow counseling. My academic pursuits are not to become a professional therapist, but rather to develop my soul knowledge (the etymology of "psychology") to inform my life as writer and artist. I became particularly invested in how the slow counseling AAP model might converge with the resurgent slow-art movement called performance art.

To better understand the symbiotic relationship between art and psychology, it helps to know a few of the artistic gestures and movements that have marked the evolution of our consciousness and psychological development. We can track these paradigm shifts throughout history, from ancient artifacts to fine art museums to the multifarious venues that house the slow-art movement of today.

Take for example, the pre-Bronze–era carvings of Nordic priests found in Denmark. The Jungian psychologist Susanne F. Fincher regards them as depictions made by "some of the first persons to experience themselves as individuals." In her book *Creating Mandalas for Insight, Healing, and Self-expression*, Fincher points out that this consciousness shift, once made by a select few, is now a common stage in childhood development.* Art and psychology intersect.

Another relic that shows the confluence of art and psyche, can be found in the Catholic sanctuary of Monte Gargano in Italy, a fifth-century altar built in honor of the Persian cult god, Mithras, and the Archangel Michael. At this sacred site, both figures were once equally revered for their assistance in conquering the animal nature of the human soul. The Michaelic age, according to tradition beginning in 1879, moved away from the ancient rituals of initiation as enacted by such cults as Mithras's. Individuals were called instead to make their own unique journeys through the universal battleground of the soul. The objects of the altar that we see today are remembrances of the more important psychological journeys in relation to them, in other words, the performances that took place there.

The Austrian philosopher Rudolf Steiner, whose work is foundational to the development of anthroposophic counseling psychology, imaginatively regarded this altar during one of his many lectures. Bastian Baan, in his book *Mysteries of the Old and New: From Trials to Initiation*, quotes Steiner's lecture, writing, "You are called upon to conquer your fear

---

* Susanne F. Fincher, *Creating Mandalas: For Insight, Healing, and Self-expression* (rev. ed., Shambhala: Boston. 2010), pp. 4–5.

of the depths, to retrieve the sword of Michael from the altar and bring it to the light."* The sanctuary of Monte Gargano, thereby, is a monument of the transition period between the world of Mithras and the age of Archangel Michael. Even its architecture forms a testament to the shift to the human individual's capacity to relate more consciously with spirit. Art and psyche intertwine.

Let us next regard the work of Italian Renaissance painter Sandro Botticelli. In his time, the *Corpus Hermeticum* was translated from Greek to Latin, and a sacred connection with geometry was revealed to the world. Botticelli incorporated images of these hermetic wisdoms into his paintings. His work evokes the many epiphanies of this humanistic era. Modern art researchers seek for clues in Botticelli's paintings to these hermetic wisdoms.**

RoseLee Goldberg explains this dynamic interplay in her anthology, *Performance Art: From Futurism to the Present.*** Whenever artists are at an "impasse with current schools of thought reflected in society," Goldberg says, they look for a "way to break down categories and find new directions." She cites performance art specifically as the medium of choice in our modern era for the most potent new directions.

This was the case in the 1950s when a collection of artists including Allan Kapraw, John Cage, and Joseph Beuys, to name a few, helped spearhead the establishment of performance art. These slow-art practices invite viewers to

---

* Bastian Baan, *Old and New Mysteries: From Trials to Initiation* (Edinburgh: Floris Books, 2014).

** Amah-Rose Abrams, "Experts Unveil Surprising Truth Behind Famous Sandro Botticelli Portrait," *Artnet News*, Aug. 28, 2015 (https://news.artnet.com/art-world/va-conservators-discovery -botticelli-328674).

*** RoseLee Goldberg, *Performance Art: From Futurism to the Present* (3rd ed., New York: Thames and Hudson, 2011,).

participate, sometimes for extended durations of time, engaging with the art rather than submitting to the common role of a passive patron.

Concurrent with the performance art movement, some psychologists began to lay the foundation for a praxis that incorporated the value of personal meanings, spiritual aspirations, and the phenomena of "creativity, free will, and positive human potential." In essence, the art of living was being explored, from Rollo May's existentialism to Viktor Frankl's *Search for Meaning*. As well, a Humanistic Psychology developed out of which the subfield of Transpersonal Psychology was born; both highly regard the spiritual nature of the human psyche.

In successive years, however, these interactions between psychology and art languished. By the early 1980s, the theories and practices of creative expression and self-actualization as found in performance art ceased their rise in influence and were often marginalized despite having great promise in earlier decades. They are still aberrant to most traditional schools of psychotherapy and fine art today.

One of the reasons for this rejection by the mainstream is that their process is slow. The status quo of both the arts and psychology generally seeks something fast, a concept, a diagnosis, a label, whereas the performance artist/psychologist knows that existence (May) and meaning (Frankl) and presence makes for an authentic and earnest form of art more suited to our times. In contrast, the traditional artist and psychologist, now confirmed that they are separate, seem impatient.

Despite, or rather in response to, this pervading impatience, many artists are returning to slow-art forms. Picking up where pioneers of the movement left off, contemporary artists like James Turrell and Marina Abramovic, are once again being featured in the art world, this time more prominently. Younger artists such as Brennan Gerard and Ryan Kelly are following suit. Each of their respective slow-art works continue to "blur the line" between art, psychology, and life. To understand normal development, and to understand psychopathology, the artist offers something important. This movement is proving powerful enough to influence greater institutions.

Since 2011, five pieces of art are featured each year in Poland on "Slow-Art Day." Patrons are encouraged to experience each for one hour. According to a report by Beata Krakowiak, a professor at the University of Lodz, these exhibitions enable us as viewers to value and preserve our cultural assets cognitively while "satisfying our spiritual, nonmaterial needs." She further states that the idea is "to savor art and learn through contemplation, contact, and conversation."[*]

In response to these new approaches to art, and a common shift in culture, new life billows into the research and practices of humanistic and transpersonal psychology. AAP's Anthroposophic Counseling Psychology Program exemplifies this, and interestingly enough reflects similar qualities found in the slow-art movement. By supplementing lectures and reading assignments with group and individual conversation, as well as art-therapy, movement, and journal exercises, AAP intends to bring people into deeper conversation with their selves and others, as a kind of patient, long performance piece. The pace of their training is slow, owing to a number of esoteric concepts they hope to relate,

---

[*] Beata Krakowiak, "Museums in Cultural Tourism in Poland," 2/23/2013 (30–31).

such as a sense of "relationality" that goes beyond material relationship. "Esoteric" by its nature requires a slow pace, as the concepts and experiences therein seem beyond our everyday routine in order to bring one back in touch with the phenomena of the mundane.

To this end, students are encouraged to develop a lived experience of the work before applying it in the client–counselor setting. The first year is broken down into three week-long modules that emphasize "Personal Self and Self-discovery." These activities are meant to acquaint a student with both the concept of a Self and the Self's own unique dynamics with Other.

One such activity from the first year of this program served to reveal the bridge between slow art and slow counseling that I was curious to explore. I have referenced the work of Sandro Botticelli. Prior to the training with AAP, I often found myself contemplating Botticelli's fifteenth century painting "Primavera," also known as "Allegory of Spring." Although the painting is frequently written about, my interest was unacademic (intentionally) and, given my hectic schedule, at times even felt quixotic. Any attempt to turn my contemplation of "Primavera" into a rational endeavor would cause me to lose immediately the mood of its creation. Ultimately, I could not, or would not, unpack it through analysis, even an analysis infused with a deep appreciation.

Owen Barfield describes this mode of critical perception in his book, *Poetic Diction: A Study of Meaning*, "The absolute rational principle is that which makes conscious of poetry but cannot create it; the poetic principle is that which creates poetry but cannot make conscious of it."* In this case,

---

* Owen Barfield, *Poetic Diction: A Study of Meaning* (Middletown, CT: Wesleyan University, 1973), p. 103.

I allowed the poetry of "Primavera" to live within me, as a riddle, until somehow I could "make conscious" its alchemical nature.

This finally occurred during the second seminar of Anthroposophic Counseling Psychology. The class was divided into groups of four to embody a section of this same Botticelli painting. With the help of a trained eurythmist, a type of performance-art therapist, we emulated the gestures of the Three Graces depicted at the left of the core figure, "Primavera" or Spring herself.

For those unfamiliar with the painting, the Three Graces stand in conversation with one another, arms threaded together. The anthroposophical translation regards these graces as soul forces. The Grace of Willing streams from the future, a sense of destiny of impulses to act based on what is coming. She stands with her back toward the viewer, reaching down into the depths further than the others. She engages in a concentrated gaze with the Grace of Thinking on the left, who derives her understanding of the world from past experiences. Thinking reaches her hand up into the heights accessible by soaring thoughts, higher than the others. The mediator of these two channels, the Grace of Feeling flows between them, in the present moment where feelings are the most rich and real. The tension between the Grace of Thinking and the Grace of Willing is mollified, interpreted, and transformed through the emotional life of the present. This realm of feeling and its power in the present governs performance art. In the AAP exercise, the fourth participant observes the three as the "I," what Botticelli intended for the viewer. The interchanges vary from strong to subtle, yet always dynamic. Performance art brings past and future together into this moment here now.

The experience of enacting these was phenomenal. By embodying the governing forces that often entangle me, I began to recognize their signatures and powers. Specifically, I identified where my thoughts of past artistic projects oscillated between working alone and with others, the irresolvable conflict owing to a distrust in my willful determination to find a more fluid way to do both. What ultimately moderated the two was a particular feeling of loneliness that happens to connect me to my spiritual path. Seeing this portrayed physically in the moment of our performance-art exercise, and participating in it, confirmed for me the importance of slow art as a method of transforming psyche.

My consciousness shifted to accept a new form of initiation, namely, one that introduces conscious ritual to the individualized soul born in the context of the Michaelic era. Unlike prescribed cult rites and unlike performance art that is undirected and random, conscious rituals honor the uniqueness of a known Self further discovering itself. Thus, my solitary contemplation of "Primavera," for instance, was transmuted into a deeper knowing of Self through the sacred nature of group participation.

This APP training approach felt in line with the methods I had developed for integrating slow art into my lesson plans as a polarity therapy instructor. Serving as both visual and kinesthetic aids they could effectively impress the delicate nature of the energetic fields with which we were working. Using the film or still version of Ulay and Abramovic's *Rest Energy* (1980), for example, I would start a class dialogue about the importance of building a trusting rapport with one's client and demonstrate how this translates into the physical dynamics throughout the session and beyond.

Rest Energy depicts two artists holding a crossbow between them, arrow poised, both relying on one another's body weight and presence to secure their positions. Taken as a metaphor or a literal amplification, the piece reflects a reciprocal participation between two people, an imperative for client and therapist, while honoring the fine tensions that govern our relationships. In kind, the sheer act of sharing this film with the students met my need to explore the boundaries between art and life whenever possible while creating a thrilling atmosphere that kept them engaged with otherwise dry or seemingly abstract course material.

The communications theorist Marshall McLuhan once wrote, "The medium is the message."* The medium of slow, therapeutic performance art enabled me to disentangle the channels of soul knowledge that I long to share as a writer and artist. The combination of rituals, performance, art history, and psychology have brought an awareness of these mediums into my consciousness. Therein lies the difference between relationship and relationality. Be it a work of art or an insight of Self, relationship brings us awareness, whereas relationality has the potential to shift our consciousness. The recapitulation of these participatory movements from our past in relation to the gift of the Grace of Willing streaming from the future marks a paradigm shift from conventional art and psychology. Claire Bishop of CUNY Graduate Center calls this paradigm shift a consciousness of our "position as historical subjects capable of producing change."** This is my dedication.

One final personal account that relates to this slow-art–slow-counseling convergence comes from outside of the

---

* Marshall McLuhan, *The Medium Is the Message* (Cambridge, MA: MIT, 1964).

** Claire Bishop, *Artificial Hells: Participatory Art and the Politics of Spectatorship* (New York: Verso, 2012), p. 226.

classroom in a performance art piece I created called *Commitment or You & Me* (2008). This project, however therapeutic, is not to be classified as art therapy in the traditional sense, which often uses artistic techniques to elicit a predetermined outcome. On the contrary, this performance moved through me as a result of an inner conflict, that I now identify as existing between the afore mentioned Three Graces.

In the performance, a petite man in black sits with his back to the observer (the "I"). He holds the place of the Will, struggling to individuate from the paradoxical demands of a lover as commonly impressed upon the observer's super ego. From the side, a woman approaches him and connects a thick strap to his chair. Her 1950s housewife attire evokes the streams of the past, and the constraining thoughts that accompany this era, as she proceeds to encircle and slowly bind him in place. Then the woman spontaneously changes. Her hair more animalistic, her dress considerably more revealing, she begins to moderate the ritual with a playful but menacing feeling. The Will is fixed, as the observer is given images that oscillate between the archetypes of the obedient madonna and the voluptuary Jezebel. This new woman, the grace of Feeling, embodies a fluidity that enables her to reverse the direction of the bind. Ultimately, the grace of past thoughts, despite an appearance of self-satisfaction, is defeated and takes the man's bound seat.

Each role is played out by the same woman.

The preceding reversals expressed my Self's entrapment. By identifying too strongly with the subtle natures of willing, thinking, and feeling, my evolving being was dizzied by inundating demands and options. Furthermore, similar to the ideal client and therapist regard proposed in slow counseling, the equanimity I had with the director of photography provided a reciprocal participation that allowed me to become a conduit for the soul forces speaking to me.

In this way, performance art offers a marker for my own shifts in consciousness and psychological development as well as a ritual through which I continue to better understand and distinguish between Self and Other. As said previously, this is the intention behind the slow process of the AAP training. That said, the layperson should be warned that too much direction in performance lends itself to theater and in slow counseling it can translate into scripted techniques that rush or predetermine the soul's process. Thus, retrospectively speaking, my histories in both polarity therapy and performance, while apparently divergent to many of my peers, have led me to the precise act of writing this essay. Had I not followed these paths, to steal a line from the poet Jane Kenyon, "it might have been otherwise."

McLuhan also said, "We look at the present through a rearview mirror. We march backward into the future." His statement reflects a perception of the prominent back of the Grace of Willing and our potential to discern its messages through a life infused with patient observation and conscious participation. Conclusively, since our history shows that "the line between art and life" fluctuates with our psychological development, this new paradigm of slow counseling reinforced by slow art may prove to satisfy "our spiritual, nonmaterial needs" indicating the development of a soul present for the fine art of living.

A Physiotherapist Goes Slow

By Dave Heap
in conversation with David Tresemer

DT: You've spoken of working with highly motivated
       people under twenty-five years old at the Australian
       Defense Force. How does this experience contrast
       with working with people whose average age was
       eighty-five years old?

DH: Most of the time when you're treating people, you
       have goals in mind. I always have short-term or long-
       term or both. At an elder-care facility, there are no
       goals. There are no goals. The twenty-five-year-olds
       are going into Special Services or dog handling or
       high alert. They have many goals and are impatient to
       achieve them. At the elder-care facility, the residents
       don't have goals; they're seen as "old" people and
       basically they are there to die. You can't use normal
       physio[therapy] on them, the medical physio model
       of testing, assessing, and treating. You have to use a
       complete holistic approach for each individual. I say
       repeatedly, "I'm talking about you as an individual,
       not as a diagnosis." It's not, "Hello, Mr. Jones, I'm
       the physio. I need to assess you; lie down on the table.
       We'll have you out of here in ten minutes." You say,
       "Nice to meet you, Mr. Jones." Then you pause, look
       him straight in the eye, and say, "Now, tell me about

your life." Fantastic stories pour out. Eventually they want to hear about you too, which is important. You find out why they've developed a mobility problem, or a pain problem, or whatever. That information is essential to understanding what to do. It may be their last day, their last month—everyone feels that they could die at any moment. But more often it's their last years, and you want to help them use that time in the best way, rather than waiting to die. So you ask: "What issues do you feel you have? Would you like to improve your walking, your mobility?" You start them thinking about setting goals.

The facility has a very caring staff, but it's a private organization, all about the bottom line, so the staff is stretched, always busy. They provide just enough care to look after the patients, and have no spare time to do things.

There was one chap who hadn't walked for two years and he felt that he could walk, but hadn't been given the opportunity because he was at higher risk for falls. The staff had decided, "We don't want him to fall and break his hip." They had to use a full hoist for him to go to the toilet—they hoisted him up and out of the wheelchair with a chain, every time he wanted to pee. But he told me that he thought that he had the strength in his legs to walk. I started him off just with pedaling, cycling, while in his wheelchair. Then some weights. After some weeks, I said, "It's time to get a walking frame, with four legs, and a crosspiece where you can rest your forearms." I paused and looked him in the eye, "You know, you're a high falls risk"—there's that labeling again—"so you might fall." At eighty-seven years old, he just turned to me and he said: "Shit happens. Let's do it." And he stood up. He had some contractions behind his knees because he'd been sitting in a chair for two years. I had been working on that, but hadn't stretched his legs out completely at that point. Despite his bent legs, he got up and started walking. He burst into tears. He's been walking every day since.

Very soon, he could spend the day with his wife, because his wife lived twenty kilometers away. Before, it required a special wheelchair taxi, a big deal. Getting him mobile, he could get into a car, she'd take him home, and he'd spend days at home. Very simple. This is not rocket science.

DT: It's a caring science. You listen to these individuals.

DH: I do. You have to listen.

DT: What's your ideal setup for physiotherapy?

DH: The present model of physiotherapy is a small room with a treatment bed, and to me that's an admission of failure. You need an area where you can sit and chat, hear their story, set some goals, put hands on where necessary to give them a feeling of something moving, have some exercise equipment nearby, and say to them, "There are a few options here. Let's get you organized." It's preventative. I guess you're counseling. At least as much as biomechanics, in physiotherapy you're counseling.*

---

* This interview gives a sense of the use of slow counseling in relation to physiotherapy. A longer version of this interview can be found at www.MountainSeas.com.au.

Relationship grows warm; hands near touching;
a heart appears. Yet whose hands cover the heads?
(print by Nikki Schumann)

Depression: Seen through an Anthroposophic Lens

By Margit Ilgen

In *The Counselor,* William Bento characterizes depression as a condition in which the ego drive is brought to a standstill. The ego, or the "I," bears our sense of destiny, our purpose for being. In depression the drive of the "I," the movement into the world, is obstructed and constrained. "At the core of what we experience in depression is a loss of the fire that permeates soul life."*

Let us begin with the case of Tom.

ABOUT TOM

Tom is a fifty-five-year-old Caucasian man, who lives with his wife and two sons (twenty-one and nineteen years old) and a sixteen-year-old daughter. I have worked with Tom since June 2014. He came to therapy because he wanted "to get stable."

He had just stopped taking Dilaudid (a potent opioid pain killer) and suffered significant withdrawal symptoms. Doctors had prescribed him Dilaudid for a period of ten years to

---

* William Bento, chapter 10, in David Tresemer (ed.) *The Counselor...as if Soul and Spirit Matter* (Great Barrington, MA: SteinerBooks, 2015), pp. 202, 206.

alleviate chronic pain related to pancreatitis due to a drinking problem, as well as back and neck pain related to a car accident. Tom described himself as an alcoholic. At the time of admission he had been sober for two months. Currently Tom has been able to reduce his alcohol use to occasional one-time relapses and he has not used Dilaudid for most of the past year.

Tom has been married for twenty-six years. He was incarcerated for seven years before his marriage. He reports that his family is "a bunch of losers." Both parents were alcoholics and abused him. Tom abused multiple drugs in the past. At fifteen years of age Tom ran away from home and was placed in a group home, where he stayed until his adult years.

Tom presents agitated and angry in most sessions. His anger is directed toward ongoing negative behaviors of his children, who do not follow his directions and address him in disrespectful ways. During the sessions Tom talks rapidly and incessantly about the interactions with his children. His tone is angry, and he uses the F- and B-words in every other sentence and forcefully gesticulates with both arms and hands. He frequently raises his voice, and sometimes stands up to act out what had happened. His anger often appears to take the form of revenge: He described his brief relapses in drinking as acts "to get back at them" (for example, his wife and children). He recently sued the family of his best and only friend because they owed him money that he had spent to help his friend, who was severely ill and died. Tom spent session after session expressing his rage against this family and was unwilling to let go of it.

Tom presents with a slightly sarcastic and cynical sense of humor. It is of significance to mention that his wife is over-controlling: She follows him everywhere by phone and takes his car keys away, causing him to be imprisoned in the house where he has nothing to do (except to get into conflict with his children).

Most people don't associate rage and anger with the withdrawn depression. Yet an anthroposophic view shows that indeed depression is at the basis of Tom's psyche.

BENTO ON DEPRESSION

Bento proposes a differentiation of three types of clinical depression, based on the soul's relationship to a particular aspect of time. He mentions that in conventional psychology we tend to look at the past and attribute to the past the origin of our present problems. In an anthroposophic approach, it is possible to become aware also of a stream of time flowing from the future into the present. This awareness can change the way we see our past and, through that, how we look at the present and at our future. Thus, based on the soul's relation to past, present, and future, Dr. Bento gives a characterization of the *agitated,* the *dysthymic,* and the *melancholic* types of depression.

The *agitated* type of depression, which we see with Tom, does not look like depression. The person with this type of depression appears to be always angry, negative, irritable, pessimistic and critical; there is a quality of cynicism and disdain that permeates the conversation. Bento indicates that a person with *agitated* depression is stuck in the past and has difficulties being in the present. Dr. Bento: "An *agitated* depression is based on the inability to let go of the past. When we are stuck in whatever kind of injustice, unfairness, or difficulty that has happened in the past, we feel we can't change it. It has become stone.... You're a victim of those memories that unconsciously set an undertone or a pervasive mood of discontent.... The difficulty to accept and forgive will hold such a person in whatever victimized postures they have been in, and that is a depressed position." Because the person experiences the past as unchanged, there is a fundamental entrapment of the "I," and the person is deeply depressed. The agitation, in Tom's case the anger, are only reactions to his sense of helplessness.

The *dysthymic* type of depression is one most of us know from experience. Bento: "It is where we just seem to be in a rut day after day. We live in a constant sense of boredom. The present cannot sustain our interest." There is a chronic feeling of emptiness and despair. Everything in life appears meaningless and there is a sense that meaning cannot exist. Why would one try to do something if all is meaningless? This depression has to do with an inability to be in the present. Many people with this kind of depression spend the whole day in front of the TV. That is some kind of engagement; however it does not really activate soul life. "So it's a kind of soul life that is numb and numbed down into its stillness, a kind of paralysis of being. Boredom becomes a way of life."

The *melancholic* type of depression is characterized by a pervasive anxiety about the future, and an incapacity to actually bring anything to meet the future. It is often sustained by catastrophic thinking. Bento says that popular opinion sees the cause of melancholic depression in unexpected tragedy, failure, or disappointment. "Tragedy can be found in the biography of classically depressed people. However, the factor responsible for the sense of entrapment in a melancholic depression has more to do with being stuck in a future that has not happened yet. Because it has not happened yet experientially, it is filled with assumptions of the worst kind." People with this kind of depression tell us that everything is only going to be worse and worse. Their symptoms and statements reveal a lack of hope.

After describing the three types of depression, Bento connects them with other concepts and possible treatment interventions in the following chart:

Etiology and Progression of Depresssion

Responses to stress	anger	apathy	anxiety
Threshold Encounters	hate	doubt	fear
Orientation to streams of time	past	present	future
Type of depression	agitated	dysthymic	melancholic
Pathological behaviors	fight	flight	freeze
Extreme consequences	violence	virtual realities	suicide
Treatment interventions	love engendering forgiveness	faith in the wisdom of development	hope fostered by gratitude in the small wonders of life

I find it very important that Bento emphasizes the fact that no one is ever a pure type. With this in mind and, even though I have questions about aspects of this diagram, I decided to explore this typology in my work.

In this paper I present two clients who scored as severely depressed on Beck's Depression Inventory, in April 2015. Each client has given me permission to share his/her information with others for educational purposes. Each of their names has been changed. The assessments are not complete assessments; in order to be complete, a fourfold assessment of physical, etheric, and astral bodies, as well as ego-organization ("I"), as well as an assessment of the life phases and other perspectives would have to be added. That is beyond the scope of this investigation.

TOM REVISITED

Even though Tom's anger is not explicitly directed toward his past, in my view he has predominantly the *agitated* type of depression. Life has never been fair to Tom, and it still is not. The pain of the past has become a pervasive mood of discontent and it has also become physical pain.

When we explored in session the feelings underneath his rage, we discovered feelings of being deeply hurt because of the disrespect of his children, feelings of worthlessness, and a lack of purpose in life.

Tom's relationship with the present is distorted by the overcontrolling influence of his wife. Being bound to the house by her, Tom reports feeling bored and useless. If left to himself, he is a warm and outgoing person and likes to be with people. He has a gift to reach out to people, which I observed in the Dialectical Behavioral Therapy (DBT) skill-training group in which he participated, as well as in his years of loving care for his friend and neighbor. He avoids facing himself: "I don't like to think about myself, I don't like myself." This difficulty in the present suggests at least some of the dysthymic depression about which Bento speaks.

How about the future? Tom does not present as melancholic. He is more fixated in the past as it continues, like a kind of acid reflux, to erupt into the present, arousing his rage. Perhaps his anger is masking an additional melancholy as it overshadows all other feelings. He certainly has fears, but these are mostly connected with his physical conditions, which are severe. His liver, pancreas, and stomach are all under great strain; he takes twelve different kinds of medications for physical ailments. However, he does not complain that he thinks that he will not get better psychologically. He perceives that he has made progress and that he is less reactive toward his children and his wife.

I have not worked directly with Tom on his experiences in the past. I have sensed their power and avoided the past out of concern that the confrontation with his traumas would throw him back into addictions. I have tried to work with "love engendering forgiveness" and he seems to have softened a little. However, his rage is stubborn and when he takes revenge he is convinced that he is doing the right thing.

The focus of therapy was more directed to the present and the future; we worked with DBT skills, which were helpful for him. I addressed his "I" over and over by reminding him that in the core of his being he is not an ill being, but rather a good and light-filled being; that he *has* depression and addictions, but *is not* depression and addictions. I often validate his strengths and emphasize his gift to help other people, and I encourage him to get active in the community, to treasure little pleasures, and to imagine a future for himself. He knows that helping other people gives him purpose in life and we have been exploring possibilities of volunteer work. He also is becoming more active in AA (Alcoholics Anonymous).

As a result of working with this typology of depression, I am now considering starting to work with Tom on past experiences with the hope that I can help to create with him a sense of acceptance and perhaps forgiveness.

ABOUT ANNA

Anna is a twenty-one-year-old woman of mixed racial background, with whom I had worked several years ago. She came back to therapy in the beginning of April 2015 because, as she told me, since she had stopped counseling and stopped taking medications, her anger had come back. She has anger outbursts at least once a day, during which she slams doors, yells, hits walls, throws things, and ends up crying because she feels bad that she cannot control herself.

Anna is vague about what triggers her anger; she mentions the example of a doctor's assistant who was not very helpful, which seems disproportionately small in relation to her reactions. She states that other triggers are little random things. She feels very depressed the whole day. She isolates herself in her room, does not go to work or to school, and plays on her phone the whole day. She feels sad and bored, has low self esteem and feels that "I am not going anywhere." She has suicidal ideation, but states that she will never act on it. She reports that she falls asleep easily (about 9:30 p.m.), but wakes up about five times per night, and then gets up around 8:00 a.m. She feels tired all the time, but does not sleep during the day. She does not eat meals, but only snacks, because "it is easier." She is morbidly obese (a technical term meaning she is 100% over her ideal weight for her height). Anna tells me that she is also anxious all the time "about life and people." She graduated from high school when she was 18 and she wanted to go to college, but did not because "there are too many people." Anna told me that she has been depressed and anxious "as long as I can remember." She has been in therapy off and on since she was ten years old. She lived with her parents until they divorced when she was five years old. She does not remember witnessing conflict between them. Her father kept contact with her throughout her life. When she was eight years old, she moved in with her aunt and three cousins, a younger girl and two older boys. She lived with them with her mother, brother, and sister. She remembers that she was often angry and sad, "about random things." She always had friends in school and liked to learn. Her mother worked and went to school. Anna had a good relationship with her and with her cousins. She was initially lonely and her anxiety began in middle school, but then she found two good friends. Her sophomore year was the happiest year she had: she had friends and good grades. After that things went downhill.

The therapist, whom she had seen weekly for four years, stopped working, and Anna had her first heartbreak with a boyfriend. Asked what her dreams were, Anna reports that she wants to go to college and marry her current boyfriend (twenty-one years old) with whom she has been together for three years. She has asked him to wait until she is mentally healthier. Anna wants to take art and business classes in college to start her own business with artwork. Currently Anna lives with her twenty-six-year-old brother, who encourages her to get out of her room, and helps her also with other things. Until October last year, Anna lived with her brother and her mother. Then her mother moved to the Bay Area following a boyfriend. Anna misses her mother a lot; they have telephone contact every other day. Asked if she believed in God, or in something higher, Anna replied:

"I want to believe that there is something higher, but I am scared there is not." Her expectations are that she learns to control her emotions.

Anna appears to have all three forms of depression, certainly the *dysthymic* and the *melancholic* type. Her anxiety overshadows her possibilities to achieve a better relationship to the present and the future. She isolates herself in her room the whole day, playing on Facebook and Pinterest. She has plans for the future, but little hope that she can realize them. And what is her anger really about? Anna reports that she has not experienced trauma in the past; nevertheless I think that the loss of her therapist, and recently the "loss" of her mother who did everything for her, are significant.

In addition to skills for learning to manage her emotions and guidelines for diet, exercise, and sleep hygiene, Anna certainly needs the love, faith, and hope described in Bento's chart. My plans are to work with her with a gratitude/positivity journal and to find little activities to break the boredom of the virtual reality. Maybe I will also go for walks with her, partly in the streets where it is quiet, and partly to the mall to help her to get used to people. I am also very aware of her age and will explore her deeper ideals with her. I want to engender hope in her. As we look back on her life so far I hope she can learn to understand and love parts of her own biography and accept and forgive herself and others, as well as perhaps develop some faith in the wisdom of human development. We have a lot to do. Just as I do for my other clients, I will also ask for Anna for help from the beings in the spiritual world.

Introducing this Approach in Supervision

I supervise seven interns/trainees. In addition to meeting with them individually, I facilitate two two-hour sessions of group supervision, one with three supervisees and one with four, sometimes more. Usually group supervision consists of three parts: A short personal check-in, study of a subject (suggested by me and agreed upon together), and a conversation about clients.

I had worked with these interns for a year and they knew that I was attending the Seminars for Anthroposophic Psychology, even though they had some difficulties pronouncing that word. Prior to the presentation I asked the Program Director to read part of the chapter (pp. 202–211) about depression, after introducing the book *The Counselor* to her. She liked it and said, "It reminds me again that I am a therapist." She agreed that I would bring the content into supervision groups.

After recapitulating the DSM diagnoses of depression, we gathered further knowledge about the disorder and talked about treatment. It became clear that the most used treatment interventions were Cognitive Behavioral and Dialectical Behavioral techniques. However everybody felt that, especially for clients with a long history of depression, these interventions were not enough. Deeper questions about the meaning of life, the meaning of the disorder, and how to live with it must be addressed in the treatment process.

In both groups everyone was very attentive and a lively conversation followed. Clients were assessed in the light of Bento's diagram. It was agreed that most clients had at least two of the three types of depression. One of the trainees reported in detail about his work with a client on forgiveness. References were made to the Stanford Forgiveness Project, to Theory of Choice (in relation to the Ego) and Narrative Therapy (externalizing the problem, in other words: the "I" is not sick). Through the conversation the concepts of love, faith, and hope became part of our treatment vocabulary and appeared to be effective "interventions" to help individuals with severe and long-standing depression.

ADDENDUM: As this article goes to press, Anna is a successful student learning sign language at a local college, and she is busy with a growing network of friends and acquaintances who buy her artistic work.

Finger Pointing at the Moon

by David Tresemer

The ancient teacher sums the teaching
by pointing a finger to the Moon.
—Beware, beware, the finger is a trick!

You see the finger, so strong and certain,
so strongly upright before your gaze.
Now leave the finger, its unity, its power,
and follow its pointing up to the sky.
Go all the way to the light of the Moon
And find then there the secret revealed.

This is an old story.
It ends there but...
—it doesn't end there.

The Moon's bright radiance comes from somewhere,
Now follow this pointing to the fire of the Sun.
In blazes of wood that claim our wonder –
They point to the Sun, the mother of wood,
The mother of warmth, the mother of flame.
Electric lights that dazzle our eyes –
Whose power comes from distant factories.
They point to the Sun, the source of light,
the mother of plants, the source of fuel.
—Don't stop there. Keep going!

The light of the Sun, from where does it come?
To what do stars point as their common source?
You have to follow the starry fingers.
They point to a place up there, out there,
Unseen origin, though felt by some.
The center of the galaxy, yes, that's it,
The source, the cause, the center out there!
—Don't stop. Keep going!
To where, oh where, do the galaxies point?

Go further and further, out and out.
Periphery calls, as a sphere of infinite measure.
Exciting adventure, setting your mind against all
      that you know—
You know in your body, which tells you when asked:
Now turn the outside in, the inside out.
The edge impossibly distant now comes impossibly
      close
The edge becomes center....
In here, in here, it's all in here.

Starfire, heartfire, fire of creation.
The Source isn't out there anymore.
The old gray teacher knew this all along,
And smiles when you notice the glint in her eyes.

About the Authors

Beatrice Birch: Inner Fire founder and Board President, has worked as a Hauschka Artistic therapist for more than thirty years in integrative, anthroposophical clinics and inspiring initiatives in England, Holland, and the USA, where the whole human being of body, soul, and spirit was recognized and embraced in the healing process. She has lectured and taught as far afield as Taiwan. Her passionate belief in both the creative spirit within everyone and the importance of choice, along with her love and interest in the human being has taken her also into prisons where she has volunteered for many years offering soul support through the Alternatives to Violence Project and watercolor painting. Inner Fire can be reached at www.innerfire.us.

Gabriel Cannon attained his Master's Degree in Counseling Psychology with an emphasis in Depth Psychology at Pacifica Graduate Institute. His Bachelor's Degree in Human Development and Adventure Education was achieved at Prescott College. Gabriel currently works with the Association for Anthroposophic Psychology (AAP) as the Master's Coordinator, where he works with AAP participants to develop Individualized Master's and Bachelor's Degree Programs. He also works with Boulder Mentors, which offers mentorship services to youth, young adults, and families in Boulder, Colorado. He has a unique approach with clients that provides support beyond the office setting. Gabriel has fifteen years experience developing curricula, teaching classes, and offering supervision in a variety of therapeutic, rite-of-passage, and adventure education programs. Gabriel also worked in a variety of clinical settings, which includes adolescent treatment centers, adult treatment centers, and middle school counseling programs. Contact Information: Phone#: 720-939-9897; Website: BoulderMentors.com; Email: gabrieledwardcannon@gmail.com

Dave Heap: Earning a diploma in physiotherapy from Manchester, England, Dave Heap has practiced in Australia for twenty-eight years—for the Australian Defense Force, for elder-care facilities, and for a general practice in musculoskeletal and rehabilitation therapy. He has been Health Promotion Officer on Flinders Island, and led the Healthy Island Project. He began the Flinders Island Running Festival for the community—ranging from sprinters to those who walk part of the way—now in its tenth year. A longer version of this interview can be found at www.MountainSeas.com.au.

Micheal Hooker is an interdisciplinary artist, activist, and polarity therapist based in New York. In 2002 she was trained in massage and polarity therapy at The Florida School of Massage of Gainesville, Florida. A decade later she joined their faculty as well as The Swedish Institute of Manhattan where she developed her own style of integrating contemporary art into somatic therapy lesson plans. In 2009 and 2011 she was the recipient of a "Best of the Bay Award," for her musicianship and in 2013 her film *Honey 1* was exhibited at MoMA for an interactive video event called "Abstract Currents." Hooker has led workshops in nonviolent communication across the eastcoast of the United and serves on the board of a international non-profit called We Make Peace, which is resolved to instilling these skills in educational institutions. (www .michealhooker.com)

Margit Ilgen worked at Arta, a therapeutic community in the Netherlands for people with addiction problems. For eight years she lived with the residents of this program based on the anthroposophic worldview. Seeking additional methods to help and heal people, she acquired her diploma from the School of Creative and Pedagogical Speech and Drama in Switzerland. A job offer at Raphael Medical Center and at Rudolf Steiner College brought her to the United States, where she worked with children and adults applying speech, poetry, and storytelling as therapy and as a method of education. Since 2006, Margit has been working as a Licensed Marriage and Family Therapist at Terra Nova Counseling Center in Sacramento, California, where she provides individual and group therapy to children and adults and supervision to MFT interns.

Inés María Iturralde: Degree in Psychology at the University of Buenos Aires in Argentina. Further degrees in anthroposophic psychotherapy and medicine. President of the Argentina Association of Anthroposophic Psychologists. I work with the clinic of adolescent and adult patients, in supervision of other therapists. I also lecture on various topics in anthroposophic medicine. I am a member of the International Federation of Anthroposophic Psychotherapy Associations, based at Dornach, Switzerland.

Benjamin König: Born in 1976, he has been enamored with drawing and painting since his earliest years, when countless beautifully and creepily illustrated children's books led a trail of breadcrumbs to his passion. Despite attempting several other professions (audio engineer, conservator, etc.), Benjamin always returned to his first love: drawing. He is now a freelance illustrator in Upper Bavaria, near Munich. His web page: www.sperber-illustrationen.de.

Susan Lanier, MFA, grew up in rural Ohio. She farmed and raised her children in southeastern Vermont where she taught elementary school and college-level creative writing. She currently lives in Santa Fe. She has been published in *Harvard Magazine; Ms. Magazine; Passages North* journal; *Poetry Miscellany* (UT Chattanooga); *THE* (magazine of Santa Fe); and others. She is also the First prize winner of the *Oberon Poetry Magazine* 2012 International Poetry Contest. Her poem, "The Gift," was originally published by *Handsy* (Handsylit.com).

Claudia McLaren Lainson has been working in the field of Anthroposophy since 1981. She founded the first Waldorf kindergarten in Boulder, Colorado, and was a co-founder of Shining Mountain Waldorf School in 1983. Claudia has lectured nationally and internationally on various topics related to the new astrology (sidereal astrology), Spiritual Science, human development, the evolution of consciousness, and the emerging Christ and Sophia mysteries of the twenty-first century. Claudia is the founder of Windrose Farm and Academy near Boulder. She is a yearly contributor to *Journal for Star Wisdom* (Robert Powell, ed.), and author of *The Circle of Twelve and the Legacy of Valentin Tomberg.*

Parimal Pandit is a Clinical Psychologist and Certified Anthroposohic Psychotherapist; Program Director, Counseling and Resource Center at V-Excel Educational Trust, Chennai, India. She has been working in the field of clinical psychology and psychotherapy since 1995. Her work experience is as diverse as the cities and populations with whom she has worked—from Pun, to Mumbai, and currently Chennai. Her current work, very inspired by Anthroposophy, is mainly working with parents of children with special needs, with teachers, with young adults in the corporate sector, and with people going through midlife crisis using traditional psychotherapy augmented by art and biography. Contact: parimalpandit18@gmail.com.

Heidi Rose Robbins' first book of poetry, *This Beckoning Ceaseless Beauty,* was released to enthusiastic reviews in 2013. In addition to her work as a poet, Heidi has supported many men and women through life transitions as an esoteric astrologer and as the leader of Radiant Life retreats, in which she teaches women how to live fuller, more expressive, and courageously loving lives. She's a founding member of The Hello Love Experiment (hellolove.us), a radical ongoing project of naming, embodying, and realizing love in the world. Heidi lives in Southern California with her husband Andrew Heffernan and two children, Kate and Dylan. Learn more about her poetry, retreats and grounded approach to astrology at www.heidirose.com.

Jennifer Stickley: As an herbalist Jennifer is a matchmaker: getting to know plants well and introduce them to her clients. Plants become allies, aiding us not only physically but as guides in our emotional, and spiritual well being. Connecting people energy with plant energy is her work as an herbalist and she offers this service in the form of individual and collective plant meditation sessions. As a feng shui practitioner, Jennifer works to help her clients understand how their personal energy (Qi), and the energy (Qi) of their surroundings interact with each other. Jennifer is currently enrolled in a master's degree program in Counseling Psychology at Sofia University (formerly The Institute of Transpersonal Psychology), and is currently enrolled in the first Anthroposophic Psychology program offered in the United States.

Cindy Taylor has a degree in Education from McGill University. She has traveled widely, living in the bush and on a sailboat, and raising three daughters. She is a Chartered Herbalist and has studied Jin Shin Do Acupressure. Cindy was attracted to Waldorf education when her youngest daughter entered a Waldorf kindergarten many years ago. She graduated from the four year Summer Intensive Waldorf Teacher Training program at Rudolf Steiner College in Fair Oaks, California, in 2003 and is now an experienced Waldorf teacher, having taught Handwork, Kindergarten, and middle school. Cindy is presently completing her final practicum for a Masters in Education in Counseling Psychology and is studying for a Masters in Anthroposophic Counseling Psychology. She works as a class teacher and as Pedagogical Administrator at the Kelowna Waldorf School. She also accepts clients for counseling.

David Tresemer, PhD, edited and introduced *The Counselor...as if Soul and Spirit Matter* (2015). He is currently President the Association for Anthroposophic Psychology (www .AnthroposophicPsychology.org), dedicated to remembering the true nature of Psyche-Logos (psychology at its roots) through relational Anthropos/Sophia, and offering courses in the United States. He writes a quarterly column in *Lilipoh* magazine on issues of psychology that have soul and spirit. With Lila Sophia Tresemer, he founded StarHouse in Boulder, Colorado (www .TheStarHouse.org), and in 1999 Mountain Seas Eco-Retreat (www.MountainSeas.com.au), sites of many slow and healing encounters! With Lila, he created the courses at

IlluminatedRelationships.com, co-produced *Couple's Illumination* (DVD), and coauthored *The Conscious Wedding Handbook* (2015), emphasizing relationships and how to deepen them.

 **Lila Sophia Tresemer** is coauthor with David Tresemer of *The Conscious Wedding Handbook: How to Create Authentic Ceremonies that Express Your Love* (SoundsTrue, 2015), whose first half is devoted to the foundation for a successful marriage and wedding: namely, relationship. She is a group facilitator, author, photographer, ceremonialist, and transdenominational minister. She has extensive training in Mediation, and has worked in the Middle East. She is an active minister at The StarHouse, co-founded The Path of the Ceremonial Arts, an ongoing three-year training for women in 1999. She co-creates programs for sacred living and remembrance primarily in Boulder and Australia. Her current emphasis is on The Sophia Lineage, (www.SophiaLineage.com), which is dedicated to Remembrance of the Divine Feminine, and which helps men and women reconnect with the history of Sophia Wisdom over the past 2,500 years. Lila has co-created two community properties, involving biodynamic growing practices, adult education, art, and wilderness in Colorado and Tasmania, Australia.

Selected Resources for Further Study

Astramovich, Randall L., and Wendy J. Hoskins (2012). Slow Counseling: Promoting Wellness in a Fast World. *Journal for International Counselor Ed*ucation, 4, 57–60. A succinct, technical, and helpful connection between The Slow Movement and the field of counseling.

Carr, Nicholas (2014). *The Glass Cage: Automation and Us.* New York: Norton. This book contains quite a few studies showing how fast has not given us more efficiency, more time to put our attention elsewhere, enhanced creativity.... These studies are each a reason to prefer slow to fast.

Dekkers, Ad (2015). *A Psychology of Human Dignity.* Great Barrington, MA: Steinerbooks. With his wife Henriette, Ad Dekkers founded the International Federation for Anthroposophic Psychotherapy Associations, based in Dornach, Switzerland. This book draws on decades of experience in psychology to present exercises that bring out the depth and breadth of human experience.

Goldberg, RoseLee (2011). *Performance Art From Futurism to Present,* New York: Thames and Hudson, 3rd ed.

Guggenbuhl-Craig, Adolf (1998). *Power in the Helping Professions.* Putnam, CT: Spring Publications. We use this book in our trainings in anthroposophic psychology as it so clearly uncovers the fantasies that counselors can fall into.

Hughes, Gertrude Rief (2013). *More Radiant than the Sun: A handbook for working with Steiner's meditations and exercises.* Great Barrington, MA: SteinerBooks. This gem of an introduction to Steiner's verses and how to use them is well worth every minute you spend with it.

Shedler, Jonathan (2010). The Efficacy of Psychodynamic Psychotherapy, *American Psychologist*, Feb./Mar. 2010, Vol. 65, no. 2, pp. 98–109, which can be accessed, along with other fine research, through http://jonathanshedler.com /writings/. This paper (and other writings by Shedler) shows that real-person, real-time counseling, including psychotherapy and psychiatric analysis, has equal or better results to fast therapies.

Sheldrake, Rupert (2013). *Science Set Free: 10 paths to new discovery.* New York: Deepak Chopra Books. This very important book assists its readers to speak intelligently with materialists who reject soul, spirit, and "slow." Especially helpful are the questions at the ends of each chapter that ask materialists to answer very reasonable questions about consciousness, mind, and the nature of reality.

Steiner, Rudolf (1994). *How to Know Higher Worlds: A modern path of initiation.* Great Barrington, MA: Anthroposophic Press. It is challenging to find a way in to the philosophy of Anthroposophy. The foreword and afterword by Arthur Zajonc helps one penetrate the insights in this introduction.

Tick, Edward (2005). *War and The Soul: Healing our Nation's Veterans from Post-traumatic Stress.* Wheaton, Il: Quest Books.

Tresemer, David (ed.). (2015). *The Counselor...as if Soul and Spirit Matter.* Great Barrington, MA: SteinerBooks. This book contains contributions from several fine anthroposophic psychologists, as well as references to the best in the field. The formulation of a psychology that looks beyond body chemistry and DNA—to soul and spirit—will bring much needed solace to many who suffer from a mechanistic view of the human being—clients and counselors alike.

Tresemer, Lila Sophia, and Tresemer, David (2015). *The Conscious Wedding Handbook: How to create authentic ceremonies that express your love.* Boulder: Sounds True. Weddings happen in every country of the world, over two million annually in the United States. It is the last bastion of the positive use of ceremony, under attack from many sides. Lila and I counsel wedding couples.

Whitaker, Robert (2010). *Anatomy of an Epidemic: Magic bullets, psychiatric drugs, and the astonishing rise of mental illness in America.* New York: Broadway Books. This is one of the most amazing studies of a cultural phenomenon, the science that underlies it, as well as the politics—an "epidemic" born of too quick an embrace of psychoactive drugs that will affect every one of us in its impacts on our society.

Anthroposophic Psychology

To guide the becoming human being—Anthropos—through all stages of development and to realize in each person and in community the full potential of freedom of thought, power in action, and warmth of heart. The original meaning of Psyche is soul, too often left behind in modern psychology. Sophia names the intelligence and wonder behind the creation in which we have the privilege to live, to learn, and to love.

AAP: Association for Anthroposophic Psychology

To guide those in mental health and other caring professions, educators, and laypersons in discovering together an Anthroposophic Psychology that can provide them with a schooling for interpersonal soul-spiritual practise.

Vision and Values

We live in a very conflicted yet potentially progressive time, a time of chaos, with potentials for transformation. To strive for a healthy present and dynamic future, our healing modalities need to address the whole human being in body, soul, and spirit.

Rather than emphasizing psychopathology as our starting point, the course designs of the Association for Anthroposophic Psychology emphasize Salutogenesis, the view of the healthy, developing human soul. We offer embodied practices of mindfulness and presencing, and paradigms to guide the counselor in therapeutic processes with a client.

The AAP website holds information about courses, events, articles, books, and research projects relevant to advancing an Anthroposophic Psychology. To access AAP, please go to www. AnthroposophicPsychology.org.